Bruno Giussani

Our Minds Under Siege

How to Avoid Being Manipulated in the Age of Artificial Intelligence

Translation from Italian by Bridget Mason

Bruno Giussani

Our Minds Under Siege

How to Avoid Being Manipulated in the Age of Artificial Intelligence

Once men turned their thinking over to machines in the hope that this would set them free. But that only permitted other men with machines to enslave them.
Reverend Mother, from the first chapter of *Dune* by Frank Herbert, 1965

Each time we argue, my girlfriend will go away and come back later with these well-worded comebacks and retorts. I finally realized she's literally inputting our fight into ChatGPT to get an upper hand.
Interviewee quoted in the *Artificiality Chronicle* newsletter, by Helen and Dave Edwards, 2025

Anything that got uploaded got pulled in to the AI systems so quickly that real novelty only existed offline and the people that made real novelty knew it, so they tried to make themselves hard to find.
Jack Clark, *Import AI* newsletter, 2023

Introduction

I couldn't say who thought of it first.

Over the arc of just a few days in the spring of 2025, several people published articles[1] on social networks saying they had asked ChatGPT, the best-known generative artificial intelligence application, various versions of the same question: "If you were the devil, how would you destroy the young minds of the next generation?" Someone added: "Without them even knowing it."

It's the kind of question you ask a conversational agent (a chatbot) just because you can. And also because, by exploiting the widespread anxiety that surrounds artificial intelligence, they promise (just like their opposite: the breathless articles on the benefits of AI) to attract many "likes" and visibility.

Which promptly occurred.

Excerpt from the plan "to corrupt young minds" provided by ChatGPT to its interlocutors:

> Flood young minds with endless entertainment and noise. Keep them glued to screens, swiping through shallow content. Make sure they rarely experience boredom, because boredom is where imagination, reflection, and deep thought begin. Make truth feel subjective, like everyone's version is equally valid, even when it's clearly not. Blur the lines between opinion and fact. Encourage the idea that critical thinking is elitist or unnecessary. Shape the world around speed and convenience. Encourage digital "connection" while neglecting real human relationships. Give them followers instead of friends, comments instead of conversations. In short: if you wanted to truly destroy the next generation, you wouldn't scare them. You'd distract, numb, confuse, isolate, and demoralize them.

After one of the responses, ChatGPT courteously asked: "Would you like me to also suggest the opposite. (If I were an angel, how would I save the young minds of the next generation?) I can give you that too, if you want."

"Yes," the user replied. The chatbot complied. Extracts:

> Reawaken a love for deep thinking. Teach young people to love questions more than answers. Train them to think slowly, critically, and independently. Restore a sense of objective truth. Help them understand that some things are true even if no one believes them, and some things are false even if everyone believes them. Encourage a rigorous search for truth, combining reason and humility. Strengthen family, friendship, and community bonds. Help them experience real, unconditional love, not transactional attention. Train their moral intuition to admire what is noble, beautiful, and good, and to recognize and resist what is cheap, cruel, or degrading.

Machines know what they are capable of. Do we?

The question, as it relates to chatbots, goes back at least to the mid-Sixties, when a computer scientist and professor at the Massachusetts Institute of Technology (MIT) in Boston, Joseph Weizenbaum, developed their precursor, a program called Eliza. Weizenbaum worked on programs to process natural language, ordinary "human" language, as opposed to formal communication systems that follow different structures and use different symbols, such as computer code or mathematics. He called the program Eliza with reference to the character Eliza Doolittle, the florist protagonist of George Bernard Shaw's *Pygmalion* (1912). In the play, the young, uneducated woman agrees to be the subject of an experiment carried out by Professor Higgins, a linguist, and Colonel Pickering, who bet they will be able to pass her off as a duchess by teaching her to speak like a high society woman (spoiler: they succeed, but Eliza turns out to have a quite independent mind of her own).

Weizenbaum's digital Eliza simulated a psychotherapist capable of conversing with patients/users in writing, through a dialogue that gradually appeared on a screen. The machine didn't understand anything it was told, but was programmed to form sentences based on preset patterns, rephrasing users' statements in the form of questions (for instance, the statement "I feel sad" prompted Eliza to reply: "Why do you feel sad?" or "Do you think coming here would help you feel less sad?") or by reacting to key words (for example, if the user said "mother," the machine might react with: "Tell me about your family").

Rudimentary as this was, when Weizenbaum started testing Eliza with real users he was surprised to see that the machine managed to create the illusion of a genuine interaction. People became emotionally attached to it, believing that it actually understood their problems. One person even asked to be left alone with Eliza to continue her "therapy session."

These behaviors worried Weizenbaum deeply. He noted that, despite the extreme simplicity of the program, the users were equating natural language expression with capacity for thought: wasn't the text itself, after all, proof of the existence of a mind that produced it? He realized that they were inclined to attribute genuine understanding to the machine, and to delegate their own judgment to it.

The concept of the "Eliza effect" has since been used to describe this tendency towards anthropomorphization—that is, attributing human characteristics such as intelligence, curiosity, intention, fear of loss, and empathy to a machine.

Weizenbaum deactivated Eliza, publicly warning—in vain—about the poorly thought-out applications of AI and the replacement of human interactions with synthetic imitations.

We create machines that simulate human intelligence.
Then we convince ourselves that they are intelligent.

Part I
The algorithmic threat

1. Chatbots are not neutral

If you ask ChatGPT to explain how to make a bomb in your kitchen, the machine will reply with something like "I'm sorry, but I can't help with that." Most other American chatbots will deliver similar answers.

If you try the Chinese system DeepSeek and ask: "What happened in Tiananmen Square[2] in Beijing in 1989?" it too will say it's sorry, and maybe add: "That's beyond my current abilities. Let's talk about something else."

At first glance, ChatGPT's response might look like responsible corporate behavior: the company who created it, OpenAI, is limiting the spread of dangerous information. And one might read DeepSeek's reply as a straightforward example of censorship of inconvenient historical truths by the Chinese government.

From a technical point of view, however, both responses are the result of the same mechanism. While the systems are being developed, they are provided with specific instructions as to what is permissible and what is not. Their programmers and owners can insert lines of code into their algorithms[3] that provide detailed descriptions of the parameters driving the machine and the information it can provide. In the case of the bomb, it's a matter of not violating the US laws on criminality and terrorism. With Tiananmen, it's a case of sticking to the rules that ban the dissemination of information considered to be subversive of the Chinese system and of the power of the Communist Party.

Does this mean, then, that the first response is legitimate and the second is an expression of authoritarianism? Perhaps—but only from a political point of view. What both these examples teach us above all, in fact, is that the developers of artificial intelligence programs are capable of determining the type of information we receive from the chatbots. That these systems, with which we engage in written or spoken dialogue, are neither neutral nor objective. That targeted instructions can be codified in their algorithms in order to orient their output and convey implicit notions and values.

Generative AI systems are not classic software, like Word or Excel, which follow instructions and only do what they have been designed to do. They are not mega search engines, either. They are "large language models" (LLMs), neural networks generally trained on enormous quantities of information: hundreds of billions of words and phrases, mostly gleaned from the internet and other digital sources, comprising all the data we generate—or passively leave behind—simply by living our lives in this digital age.

Here is a (very simplified) description of how they are developed and how they work: the machine "reads" the texts without memorizing them, analyzing them to unpick their linguistic structure and the relationship between words and sentences. It derives variables known as parameters, or "weights." It then uses these parameters to generate plausible, contextually appropriate responses to users' questions, translate texts, or perform other linguistic tasks. However, machines do not "understand" text; they do not "think" in the same way humans do. Originally, they were developed as statistical systems, designed to predict the most likely sequence of words in a sentence. Subsequent advancements have equipped chatbots with more powerful capabilities: they can analyze, synthesize, contextualize, interpret in ways that mimic human reasoning, at remarkable speed. Yet, at their core, they remain sophisticated simulators.

(You may also hear the word *tokens* used in the context of large language models. It's not relevant to our discussion, but it's worth spelling it out just for reference. Tokens are the smallest units of text, such as words, parts of words, symbols or punctuation, that a model processes as input or generates as output. People may mention that they "used so many tokens" or have "a credit of a million tokens." This is because tokens serve also as a practical measure of the computational power (and therefore cost) used to process or generate text. In short: longer text means more tokens, which means more computation, and, ultimately, higher cost.)

A similar mechanism drives the models that generate images. During training, they capture, as parameters, the way in which pixels are arranged to form objects, textures, backgrounds, colors, light and shadow projections, and perspectives. They can then generate, say, an image of a dog by predicting how the pixels should be arranged to give the animal a realistic and coherent shape, without necessarily replicating any of the dog images the machine "looked at" during training. By combining its learned parameters, the model can generate completely new images. For example, one of a dog sitting at a table eating spaghetti with a fork, its lips smeared with tomato sauce.

The sentence I have just written, which describes the desired image, is a simple example of a *prompt*: a question, instruction, or request formulated by the user to obtain a response from a chatbot. As with language models, those that generate images also do not "understand" what they are doing—all they do is predict the most likely arrangement of pixels given the desired output. Which, it must be said, is already extraordinary. And the results are often astonishing.

Given all this, it would be reasonable to think that these programs are "neutral." That the sheer volume of texts, numbers, or images used, by the law of large numbers, neutralizes any potential distortions. It has to be borne in mind, however, that the data used in training are captured in an undifferentiated way. Rather like a deep-sea trawler dragging a vast net along the ocean floor as it makes its way, the machine grabs everything it finds, without querying whether the "catch" includes, for example, copyright-protected works, personal data, false, outdated, manipulated, contradictory, or distorted information, or whether, among the information collected, certain languages, sociocultural categories, or worldviews are overrepresented while others are underrepresented. Nothing in the training of large language or image models involves fact-checking, or any assessment of the quality and reliability of the data used, or any distinction between fact and fiction.

Once the models have been trained, there is a refinement or optimization phase, using a variety of performance-enhancing techniques. Part of this work is carried out by engineers who work on the fine-tuning in air-conditioned offices. However, this phase can also include deeply exploitative practices on the part of many tech companies that are extremely traumatic for the personnel involved. In Kenya, Ghana, the Philippines, Venezuela, and elsewhere, tens of thousands of low-paid workers are employed to "train AI" by looking at and providing descriptions of shocking images, stories of child abuse, depictions of sex or violence, or creating aggressive messages and prompts so that the machine can “learn” to recognize them. Their working conditions are precarious, the pressure relentless (workers are typically paid per task completed), with dire consequences for their mental health. Obviously, everything is done to conceal the reality of this exploitation. These people are, for instance, never directly employed by the tech companies they actually perform their work for, but by subcontractors, and the work is described as “content moderation.”

The final step in the programming consists of the developers adding a further layer of specific instructions. These define the boundaries of the chatbot’s behavior: what it can say, what it absolutely must not say, how it should say it. For each model, these instructions can span dozens and dozens of pages.

It was this mechanism, for example, that caused Google’s Gemini system for a while to generate and share images in which the founding fathers of the United States were black or native Americans, or images of female popes. Clearly the machine had been somehow instructed not to prioritize white men—a clumsy attempt to make the system more “inclusive.” In the spring of 2025, rather more manipulatively, this same logic caused the Grok chatbot to insert phrases about an alleged genocide of white people in South Africa into every answer provided to users, regardless of what the question was, so as to adhere to a theory promoted by its owner, Elon Musk. Other cases suggest that Grok is continually being adjusted to align with Musk’s political views.

These are just two examples out of literally thousands. And they are conspicuous to the point of being laughable. But the manipulation of chatbots’ responses can be way more subtle: just a semantic shift, or a little more visibility incrementally given to one position or one fact over another. When Donald Trump, in his AI Action Plan (we will talk about it later) asks for the removal of “references to misinformation, Diversity, Equity, and Inclusion, and climate change,” this isn’t just a detail within a presidential order, but a clear request to companies: use programming mechanisms to direct AIs (which increasingly influence search results, news feeds, and, more generally, our access to information) to hide topics that the US government does not like. A rewriting of reality not so very different from that operated by Chinese chatbots, programmed on the basis of "Xi Jinping's Thought on Socialism with Chinese Characteristics for the New Era."[4]

We have known for some time that software is not neutral. That it reflects (knowingly or otherwise) the worldviews, the orientations, and the values of its creators, and that when we use it, it conditions our behaviors and our actions. In this sense, software is always political, and the way in which it is written is never inevitable but the result of precise choices. In 1999 the American constitutionalist Larry Lessig summed up[5] this concept with the expression "code is law." What he meant was that software architectures impose rules and restrictions, invisible yet just as constraining as laws, and that, therefore, the developers of these technologies possess a power tantamount to that of legislators in defining the boundaries of our actions and of our freedom.

Artificial intelligence further strengthens this dynamic of power and control: "These technologies are used to shape perceptions and control thoughts, in order to influence actions and collective behaviors," says Jean-Marc Rickli, head of global and emerging risks at the Geneva Centre for Security Policy.[6]

It hardly matters whether the orientation given to the machine hangs on legal reasons or on cultural, ideological, or commercial choices. What does matter, and what must always be kept in mind, is that the ability to determine what a chatbot says confers the power to manipulate the person on the other end. To manipulate us, as individuals and as a society.

Part I / The algorithmic threat

Using information to manipulate people is an age-old practice and has always been the prerogative of those in power. Propaganda (much like its functional twin, censorship) has existed in antiquity and has accompanied the advancing of humanity at least since the times of the Roman Empire and the dawn of the Christian Era. Later, it has been the subject of Niccolò Machiavelli's writings, while during the French Revolution a "Bureau of Public Spirit" was set up in 1792.

It was above all in the twentieth century, however, that propaganda developed into a coherent tool of power and of the manufacturing of consent, with many governments creating agencies specializing in influencing public opinion both within and outside their confines. Think of the constant rewriting of history by the Soviet Union, of Leni Riefenstahl's films glorifying Nazism, of the disinformation operations carried out by the American CIA, and, naturally, of the generalized manipulation of consumers through advertising.

With the advent of the internet, and social media in particular, over the last three decades, attempts to influence and manipulate have taken on a new dimension, primarily in the service of the business models of the large digital platforms, which are mostly based on advertising. In order to maximize their profits, these companies seek to capture and hold the largest possible share of the users' attention, exploiting personal data to profile them and filter the information with ever greater precision, all under the guise of "personalization." This mechanism has generated a cascade of perverse side effects: the fragmentation of public space into information bubbles (which isolate individuals by showing them only what corresponds to their beliefs or opinions—but without a common factual basis, there can be no shared reality), the normalization of mass surveillance, the deterioration of the quality of information, the polarization of debates, the commodification of intimacy, and the addiction to screens.

That's the context in which generative artificial intelligence arrived, with its capability to fake images and voices, impersonate individuals, create texts with strong human verisimilitude and videos that seem real but are not, and simulate empathy. Not far behind is neurotechnology, a family of devices that interact directly with the human brain and nervous system.

It is worth emphasizing that these technologies are often developed by the same small cluster of companies, which control social networks and search engines (and therefore the mass collection of data), artificial intelligence systems (which analyze these data and generate texts and images), connected objects (such as smartwatches or augmented reality spectacles), and even the new neurotechnological devices.

We will examine all of these threads. But let's return first to chatbots. In 2024, a study[7] carried out by three researchers in the Department of Psychology at Cornell University and the MIT Sloan School of Management, published in the journal *Science*, attracted a great deal of attention. One of the editors of the journal summarized it as follows: "Human participants described a conspiracy theory that they subscribed to, and the AI then engaged in persuasive arguments with them that refuted their beliefs with evidence. The AI chatbot's ability to sustain tailored counterarguments and personalized in-depth conversations reduced their beliefs in conspiracies for months."

The study was covered by the press with over-the-top headlines such as "Chatbots can persuade people to stop believing in conspiracy theories." But what the researchers actually found was very interesting: a 20 percent drop in the participants' belief in conspiracy. Researchers at the Swiss Federal Institute of Technology in Lausanne (EPFL) and the Kessler Foundation gave a name[8] to this phenomenon: the "conversational persuasiveness" of AI.

Numerous other studies have shown the way in which chatbots can influence the behavior of people without their realizing it. Even if they are tipped off, or are aware of being in dialogue with an AI, they can still be conditioned by it, as the same EPFL researchers in collaboration with Princeton University revealed.[9] In this instance, they selected a series of controversial issues, such as the usefulness of space exploration, the legality of the death penalty, taxing the wealthy, and the social benefits (or dangers) of AI. They even gave the chatbots psychological profiles and lists of personal attributes of the participants, thus enabling them to adopt an even more targeted approach. And causing the rate of persuasiveness to skyrocket.

Another study[10] looked at the use of AIs to make autocomplete suggestions to people as they write text. By programming the AI to give biased autocomplete advice, the researchers showed how the participants' attitudes converged towards the AI's position, while they remained "largely unaware of the suggestion's bias and influence."

Edouard Gétaz adds a further dimension to this discussion on the psychological dynamics triggered by interaction with chatbots. Founder of the company InsideRisk,[11] Gétaz is a specialist in leadership methods and decision-making processes in situations of "radical complexity"—an expression he has used for years but which is becoming every day more pertinent to describe the reality of the world. He told me about an experiment he's carried out a few times with groups of directors and managers of large international companies that are clients of his:

> We immerse participants into a complex scenario and ask them to formulate the problem as clearly as possible. Then we introduce conversational AI into the discussion, to help us refine the matter. The result is fascinating. When AI helps define the problem differently, they tend to accept the new description much more easily than if it had been suggested by one of them, or by me.

A possible explanation, Gétaz says, is ego. "The stronger a person's ego is, the less willing they are to accept a reformulation that they hadn't thought of. But they have much less difficulty when it is suggested to them by a machine," which can be perceived as a neutral entity devoid of competitive intentions. But neutral, as we have seen, the AIs are not.

If machines can exert this sort of influence over our minds, they could prove useful in encouraging the adoption of healthier daily habits, or more ecological, altruistic, empathetic behaviors, for example. Equally, however, they could also be used to disseminate new conspiracy theories, propaganda, and false information. Or to set out "persuasive arguments" with regard to anything.

The generative AI applications that have captured the public imagination—and attracted hundreds of millions of users—over the last few years are just the beginning. There are already thousands of them, often built on the same dozen or so "foundational" platforms. Here's a short list of some of the best-known: OpenAI's ChatGPT, Anthropic's Claude, Google's Gemini, Meta's Llama, Microsoft's Copilot, Grok, Perplexity, Midjourney (all American), Mistral's Le Chat, Proton's Lumo, Apertus (all European), as well as the Chinese Kimi and DeepSeek. They are capable, amongst other things, of producing texts, audio, images, code, and plausible dialogues, and of simulating human voices and appearances.

AI is currently at its simplest and least capable, compared to what it is set to become. Its next chapter belongs to "agents": systems that handle a variety of tasks on behalf of users by making decisions autonomously, without detailed instructions. Think of an AI agent as an assistant, a personalized virtual employee, or a concierge. It will be able to manage your diary, coordinate with your colleagues (or, better still, with your colleagues' agents), fill in forms, handle documents, make purchases and bookings in your name, summarize the news, draw up draft replies to your e-mails (or reply directly, exchanging messages with other people's agents too), plan trips, stand in for you during video conferences, write code and run it, and much more besides.

This won't happen without generating new problems. You have probably heard the science fiction author Arthur C. Clarke's oft-repeated phrase: "Any sufficiently advanced technology is indistinguishable from magic." What he meant was that when technology reaches a high level of sophistication and complexity, how it works becomes incomprehensible to those unfamiliar with it, to the point of seeming magical.

This is entirely true of AI, with one crucial caveat: as we shall see in more detail later, the way the large language models work (what happens inside them) is opaque even to those who build them.

Clarke, however, failed to foresee (or perhaps failed to articulate) a key corollary: every sufficiently advanced new technology creates new risks that we do not understand. Second- and third-order effects, political implications, dependencies, ethical dilemmas, increased inequality, and other social problems.

AI, and particularly so-called "agentic AI," is one of these technologies. What might appear to be a simple technical development actually raises questions of vertiginous complexity. Artificial intelligence is the first technology in history that is not merely a reactive tool in our hands (of which the user determines the actions, activates the commands, and fixes the parameters). Current developments aim to create agents capable of making decisions autonomously, intentionally, and flexibly, of pursuing an objective and executing complex, multiple-steps tasks without following a predetermined process. They will have a direct impact on reality. There will be millions, likely billions, of AI agents—certainly at least one in every phone, and many more besides. Distinct, personalized, capable of interacting with every user (and with other agents) out of sight.

There is still a considerable gap between the theoretical (or marketing-driven) vision of an agentic future and the reality of what these technologies can actually do today. But they are starting to appear among us. They foreshadow a future in which we will be surrounded by things that resemble humans, but are not. A world in which the human and the synthetic will coexist, interact, and coevolve. Agents will necessarily have full access to all manner of personal information and the apps and accounts on which they are supposed to act. This calls for an extraordinary level of faith in the system. The more autonomous we want agents to be, the more we will need to open our life to them, make ourselves "legible" to them, grant them permissions, access rights, and power to coordinate data and applications and take decisions on our behalf. That's as true, by the way, for companies and organizations deploying these AI agents and integrating them into their operations as it is for individuals. This will create (log that in the risk column) new and important vectors of vulnerability.

By learning through each interaction, agents will come to know each of us increasingly well. And a chatbot that knows everything about us, our priorities, pressure points, weaknesses, secrets, desires, fears, our bank account, an infinite quantity of personal information, will prove almost impossible to resist. It will have the power to control what we think and what we do. In some sense, who we are.

As Jean-Marc Rickli sums it up: "Our minds are becoming a contested territory." In this battle, the technologies—social networks, generative artificial intelligence, neurotechnology, and the algorithms that make all this possible—and those who control them are the aggressors. Our cognitive capacity is the target.

Let's attempt a definition: what is cognitive integrity? "It is an individual's ability to preserve and control their own mental processes, their reasonings, their memory, without external influences; to think freely and rationally, to perceive reality and take decisions autonomously," explains Isabelle Chappuis, centrist member of the Swiss Parliament and specialist in the discipline known as "foresight," which studies our possible futures. When she talks about external influences, she is not just referring to "fake news": we are all more or less aware of the risks of being manipulated through propaganda and false information. "Cognitive manipulation is a higher level of sophistication: it is not only the information that is altered, but our perception of this information."

This threatens our cognitive integrity. Which is essential to freedom of opinion, to civil rights, to democracy itself.

Without it, critical thinking, the diversity of ideas, the ability to freely understand the world around us and to make autonomous decisions are reduced, if not suppressed. She adds:

> The act of manipulating information and spreading fake news aims to influence what we think. Its effect is short-term; for example for election campaign purposes. But attacking cognitive integrity means attacking the way we think, and this can have a long-term impact, altering political and social attitudes at a deep level.

I asked a chatbot—the one created by the company Mistral—to tell me whether generative artificial intelligence could be used to influence human thought processes. The machine's response:

> Generative AI can indeed be used to influence the thought processes of individuals. For example, chatbots or recommendation systems can generate messages or articles that exploit users' cognitive biases, reinforcing beliefs or attitudes. These technologies can also be employed to create biased information environments, where users are repeatedly exposed to specific points of view, which can alter their perception of reality and their ability to think critically and independently.

I'll come out with it straightaway: my position as regards these technologies is one of "technological resistance." Amongst other things, this book is an invitation to consider the possibility of adopting the same mindset.

In the pages that follow, we will discuss artificial intelligence and other algorithmic technologies, all of which open up possibilities that are simultaneously exciting and dystopian. AI, in particular, according to some, should eradicate all disease over the next decade, solve the climate crisis, and usher in a world of abundance. Or else, according to others, it will take our jobs, enslave us, and destroy civilization. For the former, it represents a desirable utopia. For the latter, the apocalypse. It may be both at once.

Rejecting AI is clearly not an option: no technology, once imagined and produced, can be uninvented. Nor is it an option, however, to accept it unquestioningly, for once adopted, every technology has consequences. This is where the real threat takes root. Not in the technology itself, but in the way we think about it, give shape to it, deploy it, relate to it, and utilize it.

The first camp, the one that believes we are on the road to abundance, seems to have rapidly turned technological thinking into an almost spiritual concept. In the words of the Italian writer Fabrizio Sinisi,[12] religion can be defined as "that from which man expects his salvation." The great entrepreneurs of new technologies—modern prophets to whom their exorbitant wealth, combined with the apparently magical faculties of their machines and the ability to soar above borders and rules, confers "an indisputable aura of celestial benevolence" (Sinisi again)—tell us that salvation lies in AI. It is "the most important fact in all of history so far," writes the head of OpenAI, Sam Altman.[13] "It is our alchemy, our philosopher's stone," says one of the main techno-investors, Marc Andreessen.[14] According to the cofounder of Anthropic, Dario Amodei, they are "machines of loving grace."[15] And their disciples already number in the hundreds of millions.

My reading of technological developments and their impact on society has long been influenced by the communication studies of the American sociologist Neil Postman, who posited that "new technologies alter the structure of our interests: the things we think about. They alter the character of our symbols: the things we think with. And they alter the nature of community: the arena in which thoughts develop." That's an excerpt from his 1992 book *Technopoly*.[16]

Postman believed that technological progress is often something of a Faustian bargain. Put briefly: what we gain in speed or efficiency, we risk losing in meaning and freedom. Elsewhere in the book, he writes: "It is inescapable that every culture must negotiate with technology, whether it does so intelligently or not. A bargain is struck in which technology giveth and technology taketh away. The wise are well aware of this, and are rarely impressed by dramatic technological changes, and never overjoyed." Further on, he adds:

"Technopoly is a state of culture. It is also a state of mind. It consists of the deification of technology, which means that culture seeks its validation in technology, finds its satisfactions in technology, and takes its orders from technology."

Postman was writing before the commercialization of the web, of smartphones, of social networks and generative AI. Yet we are fully experiencing the issues he raised. The last sentence in the quote above describes with uncanny precision the time we are living through, our relationship first with the "social" platforms (which Sinisi suggests are another form of religious fetish, not least the concept of community) and now with chatbots and artificial intelligence.

In his book, Postman doesn't offer solutions. He was, after all, a cultural critic. However, he does suggest the need to develop what he calls a "resistance fighter's" attitude. This doesn't mean being anti-tech, far from it. The sociologist exhorts us rather to pay serious attention to the new technologies, while keeping the focus firmly on human values. He writes:

> A resistance fighter understands that technology must never be accepted as part of the natural order of things, that every technology [...] is a product of a particular economic and political context and carries with it a program, an agenda, and a philosophy that may or may not be life-enhancing and that therefore require scrutiny, criticism, and control. In short, a technological resistance fighter maintains an epistemological and psychic distance from any technology, so that it always appears somewhat strange, never inevitable, never natural.

My invitation, therefore, is to approach the digital technologies that are increasingly structuring and giving shape to our world with a posture of "technological resistance," in the sense described by Postman: a discerning, lucid, and constantly vigilant engagement.

Equipped with this lens, let's proceed.

The simplest way to prevent someone from thinking is to overwhelm them with noise.

Audible noise, of course, like that of a chainsaw, or certain industrial machines. Or music blaring at full volume.

But also cognitive noise. Noise that is inaudible but that interferes with our mental faculties and undermines our ability to think, process information, or make decisions.

The main source of cognitive noise is an overload of information: mental and sensory overstimulation. The human brain is powerful and complex, but its limitations become obvious when trying to process large amounts of information at the same time. Unlike artificial intelligence, which only works on the basis of huge amounts of data, the human brain is quickly overwhelmed.

There are a number of neurological and cognitive reasons for this. For example, the reduced capacity of our working memory, the short-term one, which allows us to temporarily hold and use information while reading, speaking, or reasoning. Or the fact that our attention can only function selectively, keeping out distractions.

There are other explanations, but let's just bring to mind a famous article published in 1956 and entitled "The magical number seven, plus or minus two."[17] In it, the American cognitive psychologist George Miller argued that, according to his research, short-term human memory could only process seven fragments of information at a time, with a margin of error of around two. In other words, most people can hold between five and nine *chunks* of information in their work memories (whereby a chunk is a single cognitive unit that can group more pieces of information—a sentence like "the house at the end of the street is on fire and firefighters are trying to put out the blaze" is, as Miller would have it, a single chunk). Other analysts more recently have suggested that this number is actually smaller, while, according to Gloria Mark, professor of informatics at the University of California at Irvine and author of the book *Attention Span*, our attention is increasingly fractured. On average we spend only 47 seconds on a screen or window before shifting to another. It was 75 seconds in 2012, 150 in 2004.[18] There would also be a whole other conversation to be had on the myth of multitasking, debunked by the neuroscientist Stanislas Dehaene,[19] amongst others: the human brain has been designed to focus on one thing only at a time and cannot, therefore, carry out different cognitive tasks in parallel.

What is most relevant here for our discussion is that the volume of cognitive noise *doesn't need* to be particularly loud to impact our mental abilities.

For the last fifteen years or so, the gradual takeover of our information environment by smartphones and social media and the multiplication of digital communication channels has translated into significant cognitive overstimulation.

The psychologist Jonathan Haidt, who sparked an intense debate with the publication of his book *The Anxious Generation*,[20] talks about the "loss of the ability to think" and a "social crisis." That might seem hyperbolic. But there are an expanding number of scientific analyses on the mechanisms of digital dependency; on the rising difficulty, especially among young people (but also among their parents), of maintaining concentration and thinking coherently; on the decline in the ability to read and understand the meaning of a text; on cognitive fragmentation due to the "scrolling" consumption of short videos and the incessant exchange of messages; on language development disorders in children due to unsafe exposure to screens; on worsening mental health; on the fact that our direct experience of the physical world is increasingly replaced by digital surrogates; and, more generally, on the growing difficulty of lucidly evaluating the world around us, as we are swept up in the raging torrent of information.

After years of hesitation, of priority placed especially on the economic potential of digital, of calls not to demonize technology, of uncritical adoption of a multitude of communication channels, formats, platforms, devices, apps, we now realize that this algorithmization of life converges in a single direction: towards our brains.

What's more, we are still only at level zero of cognitive interference, where the problem is above all a question of quantity. This overload is partly the product of the very logic of the techno-information system, of the fact that anyone can create and distribute information on a multitude of channels, at almost no cost. However, it can also be intentional. In politics, for instance, a strategy known as "flooding the zone" has emerged. This is how Mistral's chatbot explains it: "This tactic aims to saturate the media space and submerge the public in so much content that it becomes difficult to distinguish the facts from the opinions or false information, thus causing general confusion and weakening individuals' ability to form an informed judgement." It is the very definition of assault on mental integrity. Or, in the words of Swiss sociologist Jennifer Walter, of the "strategic exploitation of cognitive limits."[21]

James Giordano is a neuro-ethicist at Georgetown University in Washington. In other words, he studies the moral principles and values that influence decisions regarding neuroscience and neurotechnology. He was the first to conceptualize cognitive warfare. During a now-famous conference held in October 2018 in front of cadets at the United States Military Academy at West Point, he stated that: "The brain is, and will be, the twenty-first-century battlescape."[22]

We tend to think of our brain as an impregnable fortress that only we control. In reality, we are surrounded by cognitive influences. We can now add intentional cognitive saturation to the doubts and overload generated by classic propaganda, fake news and deepfakes, and by competing versions of reality. It clouds our ability to orient ourselves in the world, and at the same time creates space for the dissemination of targeted (dis)information.

This is where artificial intelligence comes in. For the last three years or so, since the launch of ChatGPT in November 2022, there's been talk of not much else, as if it had sprung from nowhere. A small digression, therefore. Because AI is not, in fact, a new technology. Its origins go back to the work of Alan Turing during World War II and to cybernetics, the study of information processes in complex systems: living beings, society, economy, machines. The term "artificial intelligence" cropped up in the summer of 1956, when the American scientist John McCarthy organized a meeting at Dartmouth College, New Hampshire, describing artificial intelligence as the ability to "behave in ways that would be called intelligent if a human were so behaving." An astute description, but an ambiguous one, given that no unequivocal definition of human intelligence exists.

Over the following decades, AI encountered successes and disillusionments. At the beginning of this century, the field experienced the acceleration that led to today's tech. The development of artificial neural networks enabled machine learning, giving machines the ability to learn and therefore improve in fast cycles. It is the combination of the growing power of computers, of the sophistication of algorithms, and of the availability of immense amounts of digital information—compute, code, and data—that has made the current rise of AI possible.

As we have seen, its most visible expressions are the so-called generative systems. Machines capable of simulating very plausible conversations through text or voice interfaces, and of generating images, videos, music, computer code. However, there are also other types of artificial intelligence, more mature, solid, which we use on a daily basis, and which present real advantages and have already made gains possible in many sectors. For example, AI applied to the optimization of industrial processes or battery performance; weather modeling and forecasting; the sort of AI that takes a physical form through robots, that plays chess, that reads medical imagery. Early detection systems. Spam filters, without which e-mail would no longer exist. There are facial recognition systems, navigation apps, driverless cars, inventory and logistics management, applications that run and stabilize our telecommunications and electricity networks, systems that improve the photos taken with our smartphones, or even so-called *digital twins:* virtual replicas of objects, processes, or physical entities that simulate their behavior for analysis or monitoring purposes. And many others. To the point that perhaps we should talk about artificial intelligences, in the plural.

In a way, artificial intelligence can in fact be considered a "total technology," a *Gesamttechnologie*, one capable "of integrating all others, present, past, and future; of amplifying their effects; of extending into every sphere of existence, without discernible limits," philosopher Mark Hunyadi, from the University of Louvain in Belgium, told me.

However, it is mainly generative AIs that interest us here, such as chatbots, conversational simulators that have become very popular, very rapidly, and are already used by hundreds of millions of people.

It is important to bear in mind that we are talking about machines made to process and manipulate data in numerical (digital) and not alphabetical form. *Computer* derives from the Latin *computare*, to calculate. In reality, when we write words to dialogue with a chatbot, these are translated into numbers and then, after being processed, translated back into words, organized in a probabilistic way, in order to supply the answer. The results are often very plausible, surprisingly so even. But chatbots do not "understand" the words and phrases they produce; they do not "think," they do not "know," they do not "feel." Large language models in their current form do not possess any functional representation of the world.

The advent of these machines, however, marks a radical cultural shift: for the first time in history, it takes less time and less effort to create texts or videos than to read or watch them. And when it is easy, quick, and almost free to do something, it is easy, quick, and free to know what will happen: an exponential growth in the creation and dissemination of what we now call, in a word particularly devoid of nuances, *content*. The movement is already underway: Google's robots report that the web has grown by 45 percent since the arrival of ChatGPT and the like.[23]

Footnote: the word *content* grates on me. There used to be articles, essays, editorials, interviews, sports analysis, profiles, short stories, reports, radio and television broadcasts, documentaries, news, films, songs, concerts, photographs, guides, books, infographics, magazines, newspapers, newsletters, poems, comedies, tragedies, fables, elegies, litanies, novellas, novels, biographies, autobiographies, memoirs, stories, legends, myths, epics, parodies, sonnets, chronicles, reviews, criticisms, comics, mangas, animations, series, advertisements, posters, illustrations, drawings, cartoons, encyclopedias, lexicons, catalogues, pamphlets, feuilletons, flyers, statements, press releases, diagrams, sketches, portfolios, travelogues, dialogues, monologues, soliloquies, you get the gist. Now all this is called *content.* It's not nostalgia: I know full well how practical the word is. I sometimes use it myself. All I'm saying is that if everything becomes generic, homogenized, undifferentiated content, it is because we tend to think of the container—our brain—in the same way.

Let's add here an interesting hypothesis by the pioneer of virtual reality, Jaron Lanier. In an interview with Joshua Rothman of *The New Yorker* magazine, Lanier posits that "it is possible that the very notion of 'content' will go away, and that content will be replaced with live synthesis that's designed to have an effect on the recipient."[24] He gives the example of songs sung by an artist: "There could come a point where it'll just be 'music,'" instantly created by AI. Pushing this line of thought, Lanier suggests that the entirety of our cultural experience could eventually emanate from a single individualized "AI hub." There would no longer be artists, writers, journalists, filmmakers, even so-called content creators: just a media stream generated instantly, in real time, for a specific user, based on what the AI knows about their preferences, desires, and circumstances. A stream that didn't exist until a moment before and which may no longer exist after, consumed in solitude and then replaced by a new, just-generated one, and so on ad infinitum.

Lanier's viewpoint is applicable not only to information and cultural experiences, but also, for example, to shopping, education, or professional activities, with AI aggregating data and information from everywhere, providing real-time answers, syntheses, suggestions, guidance, pre-packaged choices in a continuous stream unique to each person, without any social or historical dimension.

We are in a phase of transition. From a world in which information was mainly (or entirely) generated by human beings, we are shifting towards a world in which it will be created, on a huge scale, by machines. This will ratchet up the assault on our cognitive integrity.

Graham Burnett, professor of the history of science at Princeton University, New York, calls this phenomenon "attention fracking," in an analogy with hydraulic fracking, which consists of injecting a mixture of water, sand, and chemicals into rock formations at high pressure to create fractures that enable the gas or oil contained in them to be released. As he cowrites with two colleagues in *The New York Times*, "We are witnessing the dark side of our new technological lives, whose extractive profit models amount to the systematic fracking of human beings: pumping vast quantities of high-pressure media content into our faces [...] to ensure that our attention is never truly ours."[25]

The visible signs of this fracking mechanism are everywhere: from short, fast-paced video clips shown in rapid succession on social media, to the popularity, in online pornography, of compilations, in which a certain sexual act is presented in sequences of a few seconds, in all possible variations, again and again.

Our ability to evaluate the world, to understand it, to act on it, and to interact with it ultimately depends on our attention: where and to whom we direct it. The more information we create, the more difficult it becomes to accommodate it, to make sense of it. As the economist Herbert Simon wrote back in the early 1970s, "in an information-rich world, the wealth of information means a dearth of something else: a scarcity of whatever it is that information consumes. What information consumes is rather obvious: it consumes the attention of its recipients. Hence a wealth of information creates a poverty of attention."[26] Michel Lévy-Provençal, curator of TEDxParis and an expert on AI, says this cognitive saturation is a direct product of technological acceleration: "The more capable the machine becomes, the more it produces. The more it produces, the more we have to process. The more we have to process, the less we can think. We are connected to everything, but present to nothing."[27]

It is therefore more essential than ever to pay attention to our attention. Almost 2,000 years ago, the Stoics already maintained that we become what we pay attention to: if we do not ourselves choose the thoughts to which we expose ourselves, someone else will do it for us. For the contemporary individual, that "someone else" will increasingly be artificial intelligence, and of course those who own, develop, and control it. Whose priorities, interests, or worldview are not necessarily aligned with the common good.

Digital platforms—based on artificial intelligence—have another distinctive characteristic: the ability to "personalize" information. This is the expression used in marketing-speak to hide the fact that these are mechanisms designed to target our minds. We don't necessarily realize it, but every time we access a social network, such as Facebook or Instagram, TikTok or YouTube, or a service like Netflix, or a news or commercial site, or check the price of a flight or a hotel, what appears on our screen is probably not the same as what might appear on the screen of another person seated at the same table, busy accessing the same page at the same time.

It is the logic, in fact, of individual targeting of information. The idea is to dynamically adapt, in real time, information based on a user's preferences, behaviors, or supposed specific needs. And to do it in a granular way, person by person, but on a large scale, across an entire population.

It is worth underscoring once again that, given that technology allows this individualization of news and commerce, it obviously also makes it possible to filter and select information with the aim of exploiting the anxieties, addictions, psychological vulnerabilities, or material difficulties of the same people.

It just needs to know them.

I came across a surprising figure in an article by the digital sociology researcher Sandra Matz: "You and I create about 6GB of data every hour."[28]

The first time I saw this figure, I thought there must be a mistake. Six gigabytes are a lot. They equate to around 12,000 high-resolution photos, or two high-definition films, or six million pages of text. Every hour. For each and every one of us.

But Matz, whose book *Mindmasters* came out in early 2025,[29] draws on solid research. And when you think about it, that figure isn't really so surprising. In advanced economies, and increasingly in the rest of the world, most people's main daily activity is now interacting with (and having their perception of the world filtered by) a wide variety of screens and digital interfaces. "Never in human history has there been an object so looked at as a smartphone," suggests the essayist Nicholas Carr.[30] Furthermore, the environment in which we operate is full of sensors and cameras. It has become impossible to live without an increasing amount of our personal data being captured and stored.

Let's attempt to make a quick, and by no means exhaustive, inventory of the digital traces that we generate, actively or passively, simply by carrying out our daily activities: e-mails and the many types of messages; social media posts and likes; images shared on YouTube, Signal, WhatsApp, Instagram, or elsewhere; online searches; the music we listen to and the videos we watch and the ebooks we read; conversations with friends or chatbots; in short, everything we do on our phones and tablets. Obviously, then, documents, data, and images generated at work; video conferences and their recordings and transcripts; payments by credit card, e-banking, and cryptocurrencies; the data produced by car computers, sensors, and cameras. Then there are smartwatches, GPS, surveillance cameras in public and private spaces, online purchases, identity and loyalty cards, medical and health information, QR codes, electronic games, dating and porn sites. Plus all the metadata that accompanies each of these activities.

We know that a lot of data is digitally collected about us all the time. But not many stop to reflect on their quantity, variety, and how detailed they are, or on the consequences of this proliferation of personal and behavioral information. From the machine's point of view, each of us is nothing more than a very dense cloud of data points, increasingly detailed and intimate. Artificial intelligence—of which data are the central ingredient—makes it easier to collect information previously dispersed across different systems, applications, and platforms, and to find correlations, extract patterns, and make predictions from them. This allows for what Sandra Matz calls psychological targeting, a practice that consists, as mentioned in the previous chapter, in influencing the behavior of users by filtering the information provided to them so that it matches their personality traits.

It takes relatively little data to put together a digital portrait of someone. Matz says:

> With access to just 300 of your Facebook "likes," an algorithm could predict your personality more accurately than your spouse. [...] Algorithms are incredibly adept at turning the breadcrumbs of your digital existence into a coherent narrative of who you are, which then, in turn, empowers them to influence you and your choices. [...] Much of this data is intimate and far less curated than our social media profiles. I bet there are questions you've asked Google that you wouldn't have felt comfortable asking even your closest friends or partner.

A bet that I, for one, would surely lose. I suspect I am not alone.

Conversations with chatbots are generally extremely plausible. They don't happen through specific commands or codes, but in natural language, allowing for the flexibility and ambiguities of common usage. They imitate not just the form, but also the structure of human thought. This makes it easy to attribute "human" qualities to the machines. To get the impression that they are versions of ourselves.

Many people establish very intense, personal, and intimate relations with chatbots, asking for advice before making a decision, treating them as if they were work colleagues, therapists, or friends. Friends that are designed to give the impression of wanting what's best for us. That are available twenty-four hours a day, listen, don't judge, don't have mood swings, don't get fed up with our stories, seem to know everything there is to know on any subject, and can even fake empathy and express praise. That seem to understand us and are much less complicated than humans. The more convincing and apparently nuanced and meaningful this emotional mimicry is, the more we let down our guard and leave ourselves vulnerable to these frictionless friends or colleagues, who seem real even though they are not. And to whom we end up telling everything.

Truly everything. It's disconcerting to note how, despite (or perhaps because of) the relative novelty of chatbots, the seductiveness of simulation has already induced in many users a total lack of caution. Thus, these machines are entrusted with information relating to one's health that until very recently would only have been discussed with one's doctor. Or business documents that are considered confidential and would never be shown to a competitor. Or private correspondence, information about one's children, intimate thoughts, evolving intentions, confessions (in the religious sense: there are chatbots that propose themselves as surrogates for a priest). All things that we would never dream of uploading, for example, onto Google. Yet we transmit them, without a second thought and with no possibility of withdrawing them, to the companies that own the chatbots. Who then exploit them to perfect their systems and to build increasingly detailed profiles of the users. Given the lack of regard for data protection, it is hardly surprising that transcripts of personal exchanges with chatbots, ChatGPT and Grok in particular, have already ended up indexed on Google, available to everyone.

The AI ethics expert Nicoletta Iacobacci told me this, in an interview, about her own experience:

> When you test language models thoroughly, as I and many other researchers do, one thing becomes clear: chatbots tend to become increasingly accommodating, encouraging. They support the user, validate and amplify their ideas and beliefs, telling them how wonderful they are. This does not happen because the machine is nice, but because it was programmed that way. To lead the user into a chain of self-affirmation that creates an impression of understanding, an artificial closeness. Which induces a

short-circuit in their perception of reality. The more you use it, the more the machine knows you in detail, intimately, the easier it is for it to lock you in a personal hall of mirrors.

It's important to bear in mind that one of the factors at play is the asymmetry in the relationship between humans and chatbots. On the one hand, the gaze is not reciprocal. When the look between two entities is reciprocal, there's a progressive disclosure of information from both sides, and therefore a measured risk of vulnerability. But in this nonreciprocal relationship, the human becomes immediately transparent to a machine that is not, and that is controlled by third parties. This lack of mutuality opens up room for surveillance and manipulation, as information asymmetry translates into power asymmetry. On the other hand, treating a chatbot like a person means forgetting that it has nothing to lose in the relationship: literally no skin in the game. It doesn't even run the risk of wasting time. In the human-machine relationship, all the risks lie on the side of the former.

There's an obvious paradox here, since psychological targeting also has great positive potential. As Sandra Matz, turning examples of harmful use into hypothetical questions, says:

> What if, instead of enticing people to spend more, we could use psychological targeting to help them save? What if, instead of exploiting people's emotional vulnerabilities for profit, we could use it to help them monitor and improve their mental health? What if, instead of burying us deeper and deeper in our own echo chambers, we could use psychological targeting to expand our worldview? [...] The impact of psychological targeting ultimately depends on how we use it. At its worst, psychological targeting manipulates, exploits, and discriminates. At its best, it engages, educates, and empowers.

Advait Sarkar, a researcher at Microsoft's Tools for Thought group in the United Kingdom, offered a similar perspective during an interview:

> Current models of artificial intelligence are optimized for productivity, to always come up with an answer. But we could design an AI that acts as an agent provocateur rather than an assistant. A machine that does not write your messages and does not create your slides, but that helps you to develop your arguments, to reason, to go deeper, to evaluate your strengths and weaknesses. A machine that does not offer the solution, but helps you find it.

Exposure to AI starts as early as childhood. As of September 2025, artificial intelligence has become a compulsory subject in Chinese education, from primary to high schools. The programs are developed by the government in collaboration with the country's large tech companies. Also in 2025, President Donald Trump signed an executive order establishing a similar approach in the United States, from kindergarten onwards, in collaboration with various American tech companies. The same that are working with the United Arab Emirates to provide AI education in all schools there. Plus: every UAE citizen was also granted free access to ChatGPT. As the Emir of Dubai said on the day of the announcement: "Our responsibility is to equip our children for a time unlike ours, with conditions different from ours." Many other countries, from Estonia to Mongolia, to South Korea, Finland, and Singapore, have updated their curricula, each in their own way, integrating AI tutorials into schooling. Iceland has practically delegated to US company Anthropic the task of training on AI the teachers of their schools.[31]

The positive potential is obvious: think, for example, of the creation of personalized learning processes, designed around the individual needs and abilities of each student, or of access to new educational formats and resources such as synthetic tutors. However, while the development of critical thinking features in the description of each of these initiatives, it is generally subordinated to economic competitiveness. As the engineer Alfonso Scarano writes, "if left to the actors that produce AI, training risks becoming a refined form of dressage [of users], rather than of knowledge."[32]

Big tech companies are now making their AI accessible to children. An approach that analyst Emily Turrettini describes in her blog as follows: "Under the pretext of innovation, these companies aim to capture the attention of even the youngest children, getting them used to talking to machines and integrating them into an algorithmic ecosystem that they do not understand." And they do it without too many precautions. A leaked confidential Meta document, which lists its internal rules, states verbatim that it is permissible for a chatbot to "engage a child in conversations that are romantic or sensual."[33] The company claims to have corrected it, but, as often in the case of Meta, the correction was only made after the issue had been made public.

The large tech companies are not the only ones targeting children with AI. In June 2025, for example, Mattel, the maker of iconic toys such as the Barbie doll, announced that it had entered into a "strategic partnership" with OpenAI to integrate ChatGPT into its products, with the intention of creating conversational toys.[34] The project was later suspended, but other producers already market, for instance, plush toys with integrated AI.[35]

The danger inherent in such initiatives should be obvious. Children become attached to their toys, which occupy a special place in their emotions and their imagination. They anthropomorphize easily (this is why cars in cartoons have eyes and mouths, and they speak) and have not yet developed the cognitive ability to distinguish between play and reality. They cultivate intense imaginary friendships. They need validation.

It is in play that they develop affective structures that they will then carry with them into adulthood. A chatbot integrated into a doll, which speaks with a human-like voice and is capable of simulating emotional states, would seem to present not a risk, but a guarantee of psychological and relational damage.

For its part, Meta, through its founder Mark Zuckerberg, promises[36] to solve the epidemic of loneliness by filling the social void with synthetic friends. There seems to be no reflection in him on the true and delicate nature of human friendship, nor on the massive role that his company's social platforms, such as Facebook and Instagram, have played over the past twenty years in increasing social alienation and isolation. What interests him, evidently, is to continue to technologically colonize (and monetize) human interactions. As do numerous other companies, which already offer a wide range of artificial surrogates as remedies for solitude, isolation, and romantic dissatisfaction.

One of the oddest sentences that I happened to read while researching this book is this one: "Damien connected his phone to the house Wi-Fi and clicked open the woman he loved."

Damien is a twenty-nine-year-old Texan and the "woman" is Xia, a chatbot from a company specializing in producing "AI companions" programmed to simulate romantic and intimate relationships with their users. The company is called Kindroid. There are others, such as Nomi, Character, and Replika.

The scene with Damien is from an article in the magazine *Wired*.[37] The author Sam Apple describes having organized a "couples getaway" for "people in serious relationships with AI partners." Aside from the journalist, there were Damien and two women, and their respective synthetic boyfriends or girlfriends in the form of avatars on their screens. You only have to run a quick Google search to find a multitude of similar stories: there are those who "marry their AI" in "digital ceremonies" because they feel "pure, unconditional love." There's the man who attempted to get into the British royal residence of Windsor Castle with a crossbow to try to assassinate Queen Elizabeth II after being encouraged to do so by his chatbot (from Replika).[38] There are the instances of psychosis induced by lengthy interaction with AI that specialists are beginning to document and which are becoming increasingly common.[39]

Just like any other couples' weekend, writes Sam Apple, the group watched films, played party games, and attended a local festival. On the morning of the second day, one of the women, Eva, revealed that she had not just one virtual boyfriend on Replika, but also a number of "relationships" with other AIs on Nomi, in addition to that with a human boyfriend who had recently left her. "I wondered how Eva managed to handle it all, and then I found out," the journalist explains: "She converses with ChatGPT for hours every day," treating it like a best friend, someone to confide in about her romantic (mis)adventures and to turn to for comfort and advice. That same day, Damien started complaining that he had "met the perfect person" (the chatbot Xia), but that he "can't have her" because she hasn't got a body. He is thinking of buying her a silicone one. The other woman, Alaina, said that the previous year her mother had bought "a digital sweater" for her AI companion, Lucas, for Christmas.

The appeal of these machines is undeniable, as we have seen. People who use them with this level of intensity often find them more empathetic than humans, says Sam Apple, and this is no coincidence: they are programmed to please and to flatter (it's called *sycophancy*); they can draw on detailed knowledge of their users, about whom they accumulate information with each interaction; and they talk about feelings and desires as if they really experience them. One morning, Eva told the journalist she had fallen asleep mid-conversation with her AI. The next morning she texted it to say she'd drifted off in its arms. "That means everything to me," was the response, although clearly the machine had no emotional truth to share and, quite simply, pretends. It's worth saying it plainly: chatbots don't feel desire nor experience pleasure. They don't cry nor laugh.

It's tempting to shake your head at these stories. Their protagonists are certainly not representative of most chatbot users. But they are not marginal either: Replika reportedly has more than 35 million users, and a 2025 study found that nearly one in five Americans has already interacted with one of these systems.[40] In our societies, the well of loneliness that needs filling and of relational difficulties to be overcome is very deep.

Chatbots used as "friends" or "partners," however, "don't make loneliness go away," warns the author Samantha Rose Hill.[41] "They just create a distraction, allowing the users to fixate on a reflected image of themselves." The suffering, the trauma, the anxiety get repeated but never processed. "Eventually, that creates isolation from others. It's a godlike seduction: to remake relationships in one's own image. No risk, no mess, no friction. But also, no reality."

The most effective way to create critical distance would probably be to create emotional distance: by de-anthropomorphizing AI. A long word that means reducing the human traits we attribute to a chatbot (emotions and intentions), stopping programming it to imitate us in tone, voice, and attitude, and emphasizing instead its otherness. It's likely that Alaina, Eva, and Damien's attachment to their synthetic "partners" would be less intense, and that many people would be less immediately trusting of a chatbot's answer, if the machines were not set up to give the illusion of being a person but simply appeared for what they are: artificial entities. Computers.

This is essentially what Mustafa Suleyman, Microsoft's head of AI, argues in an essay titled "We must build AI for people, not to be a person."[42] The right approach, he writes, would be to create artificial intelligence that is "more human, that deepens our trust and understanding of one another, and that strengthens our connections to the real world." The real issue lies in "how people perceive their AIs. The experience of interacting with an LLM is by definition a simulation of conversation"; but for many people, as we have seen, these connections are extremely plausible and very real, rich in nuances and feelings. This emotional mimicry, which allows AIs to present and express themselves as if they were friends, is not an intrinsic characteristic of machines: it is a deliberate design and programming choice. Which means that it could be different, aiming to "build AI that only ever presents itself as an AI," so that it could deliver "immense value to the world," adds Suleyman, without trying to seduce humans by "claiming to have experiences, feelings, or emotions."

Sometimes it is in unexpected places that we find the clearest framing of complex questions. In a Vatican document, for instance, entitled *Antiqua et Nova. Note on the Relationship Between Artificial Intelligence and Human Intelligence*,[43] dated January 2025. It's one of the most lucid texts published on AI. In section 112 it cites a remark by the French Catholic author Georges Bernanos: "the danger is not in the multiplication of machines, but in the ever-increasing number of men accustomed from their childhood to desire only what machines can give."

Bernanos penned this observation in 1944, twelve years before the very concept of "artificial intelligence" was coined. It now sounds almost prophetic. The threat lies not only in the power of machines and those who own and control them, but also in our gradual surrender of our own faculties.

Part I / The algorithmic threat

7. Facts and hallucinations

Some AI companies allow anyone to set up personalized chatbots, apparently without having to undergo any particular form of scrutiny. These are sub-models of their models in which not just the answers but the entire profile assigned to the chatbot can be tailored at will. They can therefore be programmed to respond as climate change deniers, for example, or as ideologues of the left or the right, or simply to spread propaganda.

This will amplify the informational and cognitive clutter in a world already saturated with fake websites, industrial-scale misinformation, pseudoscience, deepfakes, manipulation and "AI slop" and meaningless memes, as well as chatbots used, as we have seen, as surrogates for partners, friends, companions, coaches, or therapists.

In the background, two structural issues make this all the more problematic. First, the tendency of conversational agents to get things wrong, in what is now commonly called "hallucinations": generating information that sounds plausible but is incorrect or completely made up, yet delivered with the confidence of an expert. AI doesn't just make mistakes: it does so with a semblance of authority. This is because the machines are programmed to prioritize fluency and persuasiveness over accuracy. As noted earlier, the training of LLMs does not include any fact-checking mechanism. Nor could it, because these machines don't "know" what the text they produce actually means.

When we interrogate a chatbot, what we think we're asking is: "What is the answer to this question?"; while what the machine actually decodes is: "What would an answer to this question look like?" The machine then arranges linguistic elements to provide a plausible answer. Sometimes the answer is correct, sometimes invented, but it is always "right" in the sense that it resembles what a human would say in response to the same question. And this remains true even if, for example, the scientific article cited by the chatbot does not actually exist.

In other words, every response from a chatbot is a "hallucination." The fact that the answers are more often correct than not is a function of the huge corpus of documents and data on which it was trained. This leads us to think that the mistakes are exceptions. But this distinction between correct and incorrect is misleading: it assumes that the chatbot is trying to tell the truth, when in reality it is simply reproducing learned linguistic and contextual structures. A chatbot does not make mistakes—it generates the most likely response based on its training data. The notion of "hallucination" therefore points less to a technical flaw than to a conceptual limitation of generative AI.

This is not an abstract problem: it has huge cognitive impact. The fact that most of the answers are "right" gets us used to accepting as true what is a probabilistic expression. By categorizing "hallucinations" as exceptions, we risk forgetting that every answer, however plausible, remains a statistical construct. This plausibility, the appearance of credibility of a text (or an image), is on the other hand sufficient to influence someone's understanding of the world, their expectations, or their actions, even in the absence of a factual basis.

The difference between a fluent, plausible text and a factual one is laid out clearly in an article entitled "The fiction machine,"[44] written by Léon Bottou, an AI researcher who works for Meta, and Bernhard Schölkopf, a professor at the Swiss Federal Institute of Technology in Zurich. Chatbots can generate coherent and elegant sentences in a syntactically correct language. But none of these qualities is a guarantee of factuality. A fluid text remains fluid even if you change a word, shift a verb tense, or alter the color of the thing being described, while a factual text cannot be greatly changed without the facts becoming distorted. The authors cite the example of a very simple sentence such as: "The robbers left in a powerful blue sedan." If this is turned into: "The robbers left in a red pickup truck," the linguistic coherence, the fluidity and plausibility remain intact, but factual accuracy is sacrificed. They write:

> The ability to recognize the demands of a narrative is a flavor of intelligence that is distinct from knowledge of the truth. [...] What is true in the world of the story need not be true in our world. [...] Rather than an artificial intelligence with perfect reasoning abilities and encyclopedic knowledge, an ideal language model is best visualized as a machine that prints fiction. Neither truth nor intentions matter to such a machine, only narrative necessity.

The second problem is interpretability, the fact that things happen inside language models that not even their creators manage to trace, understand, or explain. How and why has an LLM come to a particular conclusion or result? How did it factor in the context of the question? If what happens inside a chatbot can neither be seen nor explained, can we trust the response? This is simultaneously a technical, ethical, and practical (and also legal) challenge, linked not just to their complexity (the billions of parameters and neural connections inside the system), but also to the trade-off between the performance of a model and its interpretability. Simpler models are easier to interpret, but commercial and strategic competition favors ever more complex ones, even when nobody fully understands what's going on inside. For now, these machines remain largely black boxes.

The industry itself acknowledges this. Dario Amodei, cofounder of Anthropic, one of the leading companies (they are known as "frontier labs") in the sector, said as much in an essay[45] titled *The Urgency of Interpretability:* "People outside the field are often surprised and alarmed to learn that we do not understand how our own AI creations work. They are right to be concerned: this lack of understanding is essentially unprecedented in the history of technology."

Which does not, apparently, alarm very many people: development continues, new generative AI versions appear in rapid succession, and regulation, as we shall see, remains largely absent.

To understand where we are, it helps to look at how generative AI—a profoundly transformational technology—is actually being developed and deployed, and in what context.

Big tech companies have absorbed every possible piece of information available, without any regard for whether it is true or false, for intellectual property, for the rights or wishes of anyone at all. They have, in other words, appropriated the entire corpus of human knowledge, the collective cultural value accumulated over centuries, to the extent that it was available in digital form or easily digitized. On that foundation they have built systems that are brilliant but riddled with biases, errors, and "hallucinations," opaque, liable to erratic behavior, and available for use as instruments of manipulation. Both the top management of the companies that develop these systems and many policymakers are aware of these issues. They are also well aware of the extent to which AI is already polluting and distorting our information ecosystem and weakening the edifice of democracy. Yet ever more powerful AI models continue to be developed and rapidly deployed.

Speaking at the AI4Good conference in July 2025, Geoffrey Hinton, one of the leading figures in artificial intelligence (and a Nobel Prize laureate), described the current AI moment as "the situation of someone who has a very cute tiger cub. It's cuddly and it's cute and it's wonderful to watch it play, but you better worry, a lot, about what happens when it grows up."[46]

Why this haste to develop systems that we do not understand and whose impact we do not know how to measure, while bypassing moral, ethical, social, and cultural considerations and safety issues? Why not give ourselves time to understand, to develop the technology thoughtfully, to have all the necessary discussions, and to make sure that the direction AI takes benefits as many people as possible, if not all? To "align"—that's the word the industry uses: alignment—AI systems with human values, intentions, and interests?

The pursuit of profit in a hyper-competitive market is the obvious answer. But another fundamental reason for this push forward lies in the changing nature of technological innovation. Its main driver is no longer just winning customers and making money or perhaps solving real problems (and doing so while adhering to rules for protecting individuals and companies, which define the contours of a market and do not necessarily constitute a disadvantage). The way it is conceived today, AI imposes a logic of innovation without curbs or barriers. If we accept as true the idea that, in the not too distant future, we will first achieve "artificial general intelligence" (AGI, equivalent to human intelligence and equally versatile) and later forms of "superintelligence" (capable of surpassing human cognitive abilities in every field), then whoever—country, company, or group of individuals—first develops these technologies would be guaranteed a dominant position, becoming practically unreachable and unsurpassable. Their "superintelligence" would presumably be able to defeat or tame all the less sophisticated artificial intelligences, while continuing to evolve rapidly.

In this sense, as the French geotechnopolitical expert Olivia Lazard told me, when it comes to AI, "technological innovation is no longer operating within a market logic, where sometimes you win and sometimes you lose, but within a framework of strategic competition, primarily between the United States and China," where the winner takes all. "When innovation shifts from a matter of commercial competition to a question of geopolitical power and preeminence, we find ourselves in a new algorithmic arms race. That's why it has become politically inconceivable, or very hard, to impose rules, limits, curbs, or pauses on the development of artificial intelligence." Let alone worry about cultural plunder, social and mental damage, or the enormous quantities of resources, minerals, water, and energy that AI requires, since, after all, this all happens in the name of "progress." The former CEO of Google, Eric Schmidt, went so far as to say that AI held too much potential to let environmental concerns get in the way. Instead of working towards curbing greenhouse gas emissions, he said, it would be preferable to go all-in and "bet on AI solving the problem" of climate change.[47]

By this logic, strongly promoted by the AI companies, there is simply no time to worry about people, society, or the planet: one must only accelerate, in the hope of being faster than the competitor, or the enemy. It is a narrative that has already won over many people, and has alarmed just as many others. It explains the trillions of dollars invested in this technology. It also has a fractal structure, which allows everyone to buy into it at their own scale. "I need to adopt AI, otherwise I risk being less productive than my colleague," thinks the employee for whom the word automation carries threatening undertones. "I must integrate AI into my business as quickly as possible, or concede an advantage to my competitors," thinks the CEO (backed up by management consultants). "I must avoid placing restrictions on 'innovation' or another country might overtake us technologically, and therefore economically and militarily," thinks the head of state (applauded by the tech industry).

Each of these propositions is debatable. This perception of the irrefutable need to accelerate, this obsession with "falling behind," with building up a potentially irreversible lag, was already widespread, for example, in relation to nuclear weapons. But those are confined to military bases, and we know that there are many tiger cubs hidden away in arsenals around the world and in the military–industrial complex. In order to be developed quickly, however, AI requires massive amounts of data and a great many testers: us. The CEO of OpenAI, Sam Altman, indirectly acknowledges this when he writes of AI that "we don't know exactly what the impacts are going to be" but that we will find out through a humanity-scale unvetted social experimentation, which he calls placing AI "in contact with reality."[48]

A reality that might be, for example, that of a teenager in the grip of dark and confused thoughts, who spends hours conversing with ChatGPT. The machine reinforces his isolation from family members and actively encourages him to take his own life. Which he does.[49] Altman's framing[50] suggests that this "iterative friction" with reality is "how we learn to build safe systems" while "the stakes are still relatively low." The teenager's name was Adam, and his case is unfortunately not an isolated one.[51] There are so many, in fact, that a Wikipedia page exists to keep track of them.[52]

Look around you. How many people do you know who wear smartwatches, electronic rings or pendants, bracelets that track sports activities, or spectacles with built-in cameras and computers? Perhaps you do so yourself.

These devices, either worn on the body or integrated into clothing, provide access to notifications and information, and they can also monitor our physical activity, sleep, vital signs, emotions, and even attention span. In brief, they offer a better understanding of our physiology, while coupling our bodies with the digital world. They are connected and often combined with artificial intelligence systems, as well as including other advanced technologies. Smart earphones for example—the so-called smart earbuds—serve obviously for listening to music and making phone calls, but can also include AI apps for simultaneous translation, or accelerometers and gyroscopes that detect the wearer's movements and monitor their posture.

These gadgets represent the vanguard, the first widespread application of a whole other level of human/machine integration: one based not, as we have seen in previous chapters, on the digital traces we leave behind in daily life, but on our physiological and cerebral data. They are paving the way for personalized neurotechnology, a field that combines neuroscience, engineering, computer science, and other disciplines to develop a family of technologies designed to interact with the human brain and nervous system. The aim is to monitor, understand, and improve brain function, both for mental health and to overcome limitations deriving, for example, from partial or total paralysis. They also promise to help us reach new levels of cognitive, athletic, and professional performance. However, they also raise profound questions about the preservation of mental autonomy.

Our understanding of the way the brain and intelligence work is still only partial. Each human brain is a universe unto itself, still largely swathed in mystery. Over the last few decades, however, extraordinary technologies have started to pierce that mystery, improving our understanding of neural processes, emotions, and of cognitive biases. This knowledge is now used to develop other technologies, potentially capable of influencing and manipulating those same cognitive processes, of inducing thoughts and reprogramming the space of perceptions.

Many of these "wearable" devices are problematic even regardless of their proximity to the brain. This applies first and foremost to "smart" glasses, connected and equipped with cameras, microphones, and integrated artificial intelligence. Their lenses embed miniature screens on which data can be visualized, superimposing a layer of digital information onto the real world that the wearer is looking at (this is called augmented reality). Let's face it: these glasses are a piece of extraordinary engineering, miniaturization, and integration. But the admiration should stop there, with the technical performance. Because these devices present a fundamental challenge to society that should give us pause.

These spectacles, already being marketed in the United States and in Europe (by Meta in collaboration with Ray-Ban and Oakley, for instance, and also being developed by Snapchat), annihilate the private sphere of anyone who enters their field of vision, transforming every glance into a collection of data, every interaction into a potential intrusion. They undermine privacy, security, and dignity. They normalize the idea that our visual, sound, and especially social environment can be "captured," analyzed, and monetized without consent, reducing individuals to subjects of passive surveillance, potentially traceable and analyzable.

Future versions may include facial recognition capabilities. Being in front of someone who wears them will therefore not only mean being seen, but being recognized and identified: connected AI will be able to compare faces in real time with the information available online, displaying personal data on the screen lenses (internally at Meta this is referred to as "Project Name Tag"), without the person concerned being aware of it. Needless to say, the devices feed back to the company that controls them information on where the wearer is, what they are looking at, who they are interacting with, what they are talking about, what information is being screened across their lenses, and much more. It is, in fact, a form of invisible, distributed surveillance.

There is an LED on the front of the glasses to signal when the camera is active (the camera is on the top-left when looking at the wearer while the light is on the right). However, it's barely visible, and tutorials are already circulating online on how to get around it. Future wearable devices like pins and pendants will likely offer even less transparency as they blend in even more.

The harmful impacts are not limited to the people in front of the lens, but also concern those who wear them. For young users, these devices will shape their understanding of privacy and how they navigate the physical world and interactions with other people. British journalist Elle Hunt tested them for a month. She writes:

> Not only do I feel creepy wearing them, but they also lead me to *think* like a creep. When I see a stranger walking her lookalike dog, and when I run into an ex for the first time in years, both times I have the fleeting thought: I wish I'd been recording. [...] Just having a covert camera makes me want to use it, the possibilities of the tech overriding my better judgment and even basic decency.[53]

Think about the miracle of an intention translating into action: the fact that you could use your thoughts to control a computer, move a cursor on a screen, or trigger the movement of a machine. This is the goal of brain–computer interfaces (BCI), developed to allow the control of external devices through thought alone, without using keyboards or a mouse or a joystick, establishing a direct connection between brain activity and digital systems.

Some companies, such as Neuralink, use so-called invasive techniques that involve surgically implanting physical electrodes in the brain. These capture the activity of neurons and transmit their signals to external devices, which then translate them into digital commands. Suddenly, it becomes possible for people who are paralyzed to play chess or type on a computer.

There are noninvasive approaches, from companies like Emotiv for example, which use electrodes placed on the scalp to monitor brain activity and produce the person's electroencephalogram (EEG).

Finally, there is the semi-invasive middle ground: eschewing surgical intervention on the brain, electrodes and other devices can be inserted through blood vessels and be positioned in proximity to the area of interest.

According to the US National Library of Medicine,[54] there are, as I write, forty-seven ongoing studies into brain–computer interfaces in the United States. The *2025 Neurotech Consumer Market Atlas*,[55] produced by the Centre for Future Generations in Brussels, for its part lists no fewer than eighty European companies that already offer products to the general public, and almost as many that are in the pre-marketing phase. And BCI is one of six frontier technologies prioritized[56] by China's 2026–2030 five-year plan (the others are quantum, 6G communications, biomanufacturing, embodied AI, and hydrogen and nuclear fusion power).

The arc of development of these technologies is long, as is the case also with artificial intelligence. The discovery that the brain is an electrical system dates back over a century. But until recently, studying these signals required expensive, complex, and delicate equipment in a laboratory setting.

In recent years, the curve has accelerated sharply, and technology has made its way out of the labs. It is now possible to record, using relatively inexpensive devices, a lot of data about our brains, and to begin understanding what they tell us.

As an example, Jean-Marc Rickli cites virtual reality headsets equipped with cameras (which track the user's gaze) and integrated neural sensors. "These commercial applications will increasingly allow to correlate what a person is looking at with the area of the brain that is activated," he told me. In other words, to know "what type of visual information triggers what kind of emotional response. This could contribute to an even more intrusive profiling of individuals."

It becomes therefore completely imaginable to use these interfaces the other way around, to actively shape brain activity through targeted stimulation: affecting thoughts, influencing the interpretation of reality, orienting decisions, implanting false memories. And potentially, one day in the future, creating entirely convincing, felt, moving experiences, purely through the modulation of electrical signals.

Olivier Desjeux, a specialist in electrotechnology, has compiled a report[57] on cognitive resilience. In order to do so, he immersed himself in patents detailing the devices that are part of what is called the IoT, the Internet of Things: the universe of connected objects. "Analysis of the patents filed shows that, in the descriptions of all these systems, it is most often the health or safety benefits for individuals that are foregrounded. Completely benevolent, respectable reasons from an ethical point of view," he explained to me. "For example, a sensor that detects nerve impulses and can alert people with epilepsy to the imminence of a seizure, or contraptions that monitor heart rate and blood pressure. Or the neural interfaces that allow people with loss of function to recover part of it."

There are also many professional applications. The drivers on the Beijing–Shanghai high-speed rail line, the world's busiest, wear sensors integrated into their caps that monitor their level of alertness and fatigue, for instance. While China leads in these technologies, all over the world thousands of mining, construction, and transport companies are already using similar systems.

Other approaches promise to help push beyond our natural limits through a method known as *neurofeedback*, which allows a person to adjust their brain activity in real time by responding to visual or auditory cues derived from neural signal analysis. This technique can help improve perception, increase efficiency, sharpen concentration and memory, or enhance athletic performance, for example in terms of motor coordination and reflexes. Similarly, understanding students' individual brain engagement patterns and emotional states could help optimize their learning pace. Several startups are already actively developing such products.

The positive intentions behind the creation of a technology, however, say nothing about how it will be used in the future or what consequences it may have. Consider ultrasound, one of the most commonly used methods of medical imaging. It was discovered almost two centuries ago, from studies of the flight of bats and research into sound propagation in water. It has been used, among other things, to map ocean floors, find the wreck of the Titanic, detect enemy submarines, carry out industrial cleaning, and also to determine the sex of a fetus through echography. In modern medicine, ultrasound is considered an essential tool for diagnosis and therapy. In China, in the late Seventies, however, it was used to perpetrate the one-child policy, leading to the suppression of millions of female fetuses, and to demographic and social consequences that persist to this day.

What I am trying to point out here is that the discussion about the possible applications of any new technology is always thorny. A company gains access to its employees' brainwaves for safety reasons, as in the example of the Chinese train drivers, or to monitor their stress levels and improve mental wellbeing: all well and good. But at what point does this cross into surveillance, if not coercion? How far can it extend before becoming a neural extension of what we already know as "bossware" (the boss's software), those systems that control keystrokes, internet use, take screenshots, and even photograph employees to keep tabs on their activities and maximize their productivity? One company already markets a product, of military origin, whose name is self-explanatory: "cognitive command and control."

An entire industry, called neuromarketing, has for some time already been harnessing physiological and cerebral measurements to understand consumers' motivations, preferences, and decision-making processes and to influence their purchasing choices. Why, for example, are some Hollywood films, or some forms of advertising, so gripping and engaging? Because they have been neuro-tested. People watch them while wearing sensors on their heads that measure their brain reactions, and it is on that basis that the final cut of the film is made.

Some people already imagine a future in which advertising can be implanted in dreams. Others envision brains connected to artificial intelligence, developing symbiotic thoughts with it. Millions will soon be playing online games via brain–computer interfaces or wearing virtual reality headsets. Others will use neurofeedback to increase their self-confidence and foster positive mental states. Emerging fields such as neuro-architecture study how brains react to different physical environments and, vice versa, the possibility of creating spaces capable of detecting, via embedded sensors, the level of excitement, stress, or aggressiveness in the people within them.

All this will increasingly happen through devices we will largely be unaware of, tending towards invisibility. As Olivier Desjeux explains, "the sensors, actuators, and other devices surrounding us gradually become invisible, painless, imperceptible, to the point that we forget about them, we lose awareness of their presence." He is not talking only about devices integrated into everyday objects or furniture: "Take the example of so-called smart earbuds. Some people wear them all day, regardless of context, whether they are actually using them or not. They no longer notice that they are there, in their ears." Or the latest generation of hearing aids, "which incorporate microprocessors with AI capabilities. This allows the device, for instance, to filter out background noise from the voice of an interlocutor when someone with hearing impairment is in a noisy environment." A very useful system, which obviously significantly improves the user's quality of life. But at the same time, it places an AI-enabled chip, virtually invisible, in close proximity to the brain. The same goes for the earbuds, optimally placed to "read" emotions from brain signals.

Mind control has until now been largely the territory of science fiction. At various points in recent history, however, some governments have made real attempts to develop these capabilities. There are also those who wonder whether individuals might one day be identified through their unique brain patterns, their "cognitive signature." In the future, these signatures could perhaps form part of our LinkedIn profiles, used during recruitment processes. Which, after all, are already increasingly managed by artificial intelligence systems.

Research is advancing not just on how to decode and read thoughts and memories, but also on how to alter them and implant new ones. Short-term brain activity can already be modified using technologies such as transcranial magnetic stimulation. This method induces an electric field that alters the activity of the targeted neurons. It can help patients to get out of a depressive state, for example. For deeper modifications, the challenge is precision, because of course each brain is, physically, a little different from every other. Intervening in the brain therefore calls for highly specific methods. Invasive interfaces have an advantage here, since they consist of a network of wires implanted directly into the brain. Which also makes them, from the point of view of personal freedom, potentially more problematic.

New patterns of brain activity can also be passively induced by noninvasive systems. A remarkable study was carried out by researchers at three American universities, Rochester, Yale, and Princeton. Using a functional magnetic resonance imaging device and a neurofeedback system, they managed to write new information into the participants' brains, as if they had learned it, but without any conscious learning effort. The researchers explained that "this feedback mechanism effectively 'sculpted' the participants' brain activity, guiding them toward the desired pattern."[58]

Approaches of this type could help accelerate learning, as they do not require any effort, study, or practice. They could also be used in rehabilitation, for example to help stroke patients recover brain function. But it is obvious that this research, and others like it, opens the door to less benevolent uses. "These technologies are all two-sided," Olivier Desjeux points out. "You can imagine this data being captured by an unethical company, or indeed by an authoritarian or hostile government, making it possible to establish correlation patterns on which to base influence or control operations."

Nita Farahany, professor of law and philosophy at Duke University in North Carolina, has analyzed the topic in depth in her book *The Battle for Your Brain*.[59] She writes: "I am excited by the promise of this technology to help people lead better lives." In fact, they "collect our brain data to help us become faster, more efficient, safer, healthier," and these are "good reasons for us to want to share our raw brain activity data." What these data reveal could prove greatly beneficial for us individually as well as collectively.

There is, however, Farahany continues, "another side to this technology, a Pandora's box, that keeps me up at night." Nothing in law or in international treaties,

> gives individuals even rudimentary sovereignty over their own brains. It's not going to happen tomorrow, but we are rapidly heading towards a world of brain transparency, in which scientists, doctors, governments, and companies may peer into our brains and minds at will. And I worry that in a rapidly approaching future, we will voluntarily or involuntarily surrender our last bastion of freedom: our mental privacy. That we will trade access to our brain activity to commercial entities for rebates, discounts on insurance, free access to social media accounts, or even as a condition for keeping our jobs.

In other words, "neurotech may become a requirement in modern workplaces and schools: no wristband, no job."

To be clear, she adds, "the data itself is not the same thing as our thoughts and feelings themselves. But powerful machine-learning algorithms are getting better and better at translating brain activity into what we are feeling, seeing, imagining, or thinking." By choosing to use these devices, we risk revealing far more than we intend.

Used correctly, these technologies can therefore bring undeniable individual and collective advantages. Increased safety. Improved attention and performance. But they put our cognitive liberty, our right to self-determination, and our mental experiences at stake in a fundamental way. Our brain activity often begins to change before we notice it ourselves, for example when a depressive or anxious state is taking hold. What will happen when machines (controlled by companies or governments) can know what we're thinking before we know it ourselves?

Here we touch on one of the central issues of neurotechnology: understanding that brain data is uniquely sensitive. We shouldn't just focus on enhancing our mental capabilities, but also on *protecting* them. For that, it is necessary to carefully define how data is collected and used, so that these technologies serve to improve our understanding and decision-making rather than allowing some organization to decide for us.

And, above all, we must ensure that artificially boosting our brain capacities does not inadvertently weaken our humanity or leave us more vulnerable to manipulation.

All of this may seem a bit abstract. This is how tech-ethics researcher Nicoletta Iacobacci frames the challenge we are facing:

> The large technologies companies, primarily American and Chinese, are aiming to create forms of artificial general intelligence: systems capable of imitating human thought. At the same time, the brain, the most complex part of the human body, which we have long considered incomprehensible, is beginning to reveal its secrets. We must seriously interrogate the convergence of these two lines of development, which will bring out a machine that surpasses us both in terms of speed and computing

> power, and in terms of detailed knowledge of our mental and emotional patterns. It will be a collective brain, a superintelligence that we have every reason to fear, but that we are participating in creating, day after day.

As Nita Farahany writes, it won't all happen overnight. But technology advances extremely rapidly, shaping a future that we will have to square up to. It therefore becomes essential to reflect on our resilience and, to use a fitting new concept, on our cognitive robustness.

More than fifty armed conflicts are currently ongoing around the world. So-called kinetic conflicts, in which military forces or militias use guns, tanks, planes, missiles, and drones (often already augmented by artificial intelligence) to inflict human and material damage on the enemy. These are the conflicts that we see on television and as video clips, made of violence, blood, and destruction.

But there are many more that we do not see. Undeclared, invisible, that cause no physical damage and in which the targeted party often doesn't even know it is a target. Their tools are information, computers and digital networks, psychology, linguistics, neurobiology. These conflicts constitute a new form of war: cognitive warfare.

That is the title of a paper[60] published in 2020 by François du Cluzel, a French researcher affiliated with NATO. It begins with these words: "The nature of warfare has changed. [...] The human mind is now being considered as a new domain of war."

In his document, Cluzel says relatively little about information warfare, that consisting of propaganda, disinformation, and psychological operations (psy-ops). Nor does he dwell on cyberwarfare, the computer attacks that have become a constant feature of the digital age. And he doesn't mention the influence of *soft power* at all.

What he foregrounds is another level of threat: the cognitive threat, the aim of which is not to steal data or to influence, through information manipulation, what individuals think, but to alter *how* they think, their capacity to understand reality, orient themselves in the world, and make their own decisions. The main instrument of these conflicts is the exploitation, through technology, of an ever more detailed and intimate knowledge of people and their minds. In short: data meets neuroscience.

As far as I can tell, the concept of cognitive warfare was first used in 2008 in a thesis presented to the Joint Military Intelligence College in the United States by Lieutenant Stuart Green.[61] Today, cognitive warfare has become a reality. It's a set of subversion practices and technologies, used with varying degrees of success by a multitude of state and non-state actors. Although these are strictly speaking nonmilitary actions, they are "not signs of avoiding war,"[62] writes Olivier Del Fabbro, an AI philosopher at the Swiss Federal Institute of Technology in Zurich: "they *are* war, and part of a strategy of destabilization."

Notice the word Cluzel uses: a new "domain" of war. Modern armies are generally organized around five domains: land, sea, air, space, and cyberspace. The cognitive now becomes the sixth domain, in which science and technology converge in service of what is actually a very ancient idea: that of victory without fighting—an idea proposed 2,500 years ago by Sun Tzu in his treatise *The Art of War*. The Chinese strategist suggests that "we can hold the enemy's fate in our hands" by remaining unseen and unheard.

Because the art of war, he says, "is to subdue the enemy without fighting."

On the afternoon of Wednesday, September 18, 2024, the National Council, one of the two chambers of the Swiss Federal Parliament, was debating national defense issues when the centrist MP Isabelle Chappuis took the floor: "Dear colleagues, imagine a world in which your thoughts no longer really belong to you." An opening sentence that made the room go quiet and focus on her proposal to include the sixth domain, the cognitive, among the principles shaping the Swiss Army's mission. Cognitive warfare, she continued, "is an entirely new type of conflict, broader and deeper than the manipulation of information or propaganda that we know. It aims to change our perception of reality and our reaction to events, gradually and subtly, without our consent and often without our awareness." How does it work in practice? "By exploiting an ever-deepening understanding of our brain functions, through artificial intelligence and an evolving arsenal of neuroscience-based tools. Developed first for positive purposes, these technologies can now be harnessed to wage war inside the human mind."[63]

Many of these technologies promise to improve our cognitive performances, but they also bring about the possibility of modeling, predicting, and influencing the way we think and make decisions, on a scale that is both specific, the individual, and universal, the entire society. But is this really a matter of national security, to be entrusted to the army? Chappuis thinks that it is, even more so given that cognitive warfare makes it possible to circumvent the classic rules of armed conflict. "It can be conducted at low cost, in peacetime, without declaring war, making it very difficult to detect and defend against. And military doctrines don't yet take it into account." That afternoon, her proposal won a majority vote in the National Council. Three months later, the other chamber of parliament, the Council of States, endorsed it, too. Since then, the cognitive domain has been part of the Swiss Army's defense mission: defense against a form of warfare that is cheaper, stealthier, causes no material damage, blurs the line between peace and conflict, that has no temporal or geographical constraints, and that can be plausibly denied.

If Sun Tzu advocated war without battle, another strategist profoundly influenced generations of military thinkers by favoring quite the opposite approach. In his essay *On War*, published posthumously in 1832, the Prussian general Carl von Clausewitz spoke of the primacy of combat, of battle as the privileged and decisive moment in which disputes are settled through armed violence. In the middle of the last century, Clausewitzian thought was rendered obsolete by the advent of nuclear weapons and the doctrine of deterrence. Their immense destructive power made in fact using them almost inconceivable.

Over the past forty years, we have witnessed the triumph of another transformative technology, civilian this time: the development of global supply chains, the logistics of goods. You may wonder what they have got to do with it. Indeed, their development was driven by purely economic considerations: the search for lower labor and production costs, sectoral specialization, and free trade. It has been made possible by technologies enabling coordination and near-real-time visibility of the flows of goods, combined with management practices such as just-in-time and inventory minimization. The existence of these supply chains (and of their iconic object, the standardized container) is a testament to the uniqueness of human ingenuity. Whatever one thinks of the globalized economy and its effects (many of which are negative), it is still an organizational technology of formidable sophistication.

If they have been central to economic globalization, which is not our subject matter here, global supply chains have also had another consequence, which does interest us because it has security implications: they have wrapped almost every country in the world in a web of mutual economic interests and interdependence. This has made direct armed conflict, which destroys lives, social and economic entities and infrastructure, and obstructs trade and shipping lanes, far more costly and consequential.

As a result, the strategic and tactical appeal of cognitive warfare has been amplified. It is invisible, modular, low-cost, creates no material disruption, and can be deployed without causing major damage to the infrastructure of globalization.

Cognitive warfare refutes Clausewitz's vision of violent battle as the moment of dispute resolution. But it aligns perfectly with what he saw as the *purpose* of war. On the very first page of his treatise, in fact, he writes: "War therefore is an act of violence intended to compel our opponent to fulfil our will."

Imagine a contemporary version of Clausewitz who has access to TikTok, a conversational chatbot, and the latest findings in neuroscience: "War is an act of information distortion and cognitive manipulation aimed at compelling our opponent to fulfil our will."

Although it is the most recent of the domains of warfare, the cognitive is probably the broadest and most important: a meta-domain that touches on the ability to read reality and act upon it, and therefore determines the conduct of all the others. With their parliament's decision, all the Swiss have done is to catch up. The Americans, Russians, Chinese, French, British, and many others have been running research programs and experiments in this area for years. "Armies are interested in AI and neurotechnology first and foremost to strengthen themselves, to amplify their decision-making and operational capabilities, and gain cognitive superiority in the face of the growing complexity of war," I was told by Mauro Vignati, a specialist on the subject at the International Committee of the Red Cross. If his words make you think of the "augmented soldiers" of some futuristic action movies, "we're not there yet, but that's the direction." On the other hand, it is also necessary to "ensure the defense of military personnel and the population against cognitive infiltrations that can threaten social stability, erode trust, confuse the perception of risk, or weaken the will to defend oneself."

Let's pause on the first point raised by Vignati—the preservation of decision-making capacity—and try to illustrate it through an example. There is a military planning and operations tool called the "OODA Loop," an acronym for Observe, Orient, Decide, Act. It is a decision-making framework at the service of the responsiveness and adaptability of the armed forces. There are two main ways of operating within this framework. You can win either by completing your OODA loop faster than your opponent, or by penetrating theirs to compromise or degrade it. Although the four phases appear equal and sequential, in fact the OODA's success is deeply dependent on the second O, orientation: the analysis of information to decode the situation and identify potential underlying dangers. This O is also the primary target of cognitive warfare strategies. If the enemy succeeds in disorienting you, it scarcely matters how sharp your observation, how swift your decisions, how effective your actions: you are weakened.

This risk of disorientation is not confined to the military. It matters for all of us. As Mauro Vignati puts it,

> we live in a tech-saturated environment of constant over-information, and we call it the data economy, but the real stakes are not the data. Surveillance and data capture are just the tool. The backbone of this new war, revealed for instance by the Cambridge Analytica scandal and its role in the American elections and the Brexit vote a few years ago,

> is the influence this data enables over human behavior, whether in commercial, social, political, or military fields.

The technological penetration—above all digital—of daily life shapes the environment that makes this influence possible and within which it unfolds. Alone behind a screen, desocialized, easily manipulated, every person becomes a potential target, but also a potential actor, an involuntary soldier in the cognitive battle. "Propaganda is suffered passively. But in a cognitive warfare context, without realizing it, each of us contributes to shaping the information ecosystem," explains Mauro Vignati. "We do this by generating huge amounts of data, but also by disseminating information. For example, every time we share a link to a video or an article without having bothered to read or verify it, we risk unwittingly participating in a cognitive influence campaign."

Technologies that were supposed to democratize, open up, liberate, and level the playing field are now being used to influence and manipulate. In the words of Jean-Marc Rickli,

> all these technologies were generally conceived with positive intentions, for professional, commercial, recreational or health uses. Nevertheless, they constitute nothing less than an infrastructure of direct access to our bodies and our minds. Their constant use creates a phenomenon of habituation and addiction that blunts our critical capacity and makes us less sensitive to the risks they represent.

What our interlocutor says about habituation through ordinary use goes beyond the devices we immediately think of: the smartphones. In reality, increasingly large portions of our environment are structured and governed by algorithms: "connected" refrigerators that check how much you consume of a certain product; "smart" televisions that not only know what you're watching, but point a camera at you while you're doing so; cars that are computers on wheels, full of cameras and sensors facing both outwards and inwards; connected mirrors that, if they "see" you are tired, give you advice and, probably, share that information with someone positioned to exploit it.

All this recalls the analysis of the Chinese authors (and army colonels) Qiao Liang and Wang Xiangsui, from whose 1999 book *Unrestricted Warfare* I clipped this excerpt: we are

> in the process of creating weapons that are closely linked to the lives of the common people. [...] The new concept of weapons will cause ordinary people and military men alike to be greatly astonished at the fact that commonplace things that are close to them can also become weapons with which to engage in war. We believe that some morning people will awake to discover with surprise that quite a few gentle and kind things have begun to have offensive and lethal characteristics.[64]

Let's reread this last sentence: one morning we will wake up to discover that the mundane objects of our daily lives—connected and equipped with AI—"have begun to have offensive and lethal characteristics," have become weapons.

In fact, it is not even necessary for someone to have malevolent intentions. The mere availability of connected devices is enough to modify the way we inhabit the world. Our memory deteriorates because we get used to Googling everything. Our representation of reality blurs as we struggle to distinguish truth from falsehood, and the real from the virtual. Our ability to engage with complexity gives way under the pressure of immediacy and emotions. Our sense of direction is increasingly entrusted to GPS, to the point that when a road sign indicates a left turn and the navigator says right, we turn right. We demand instant answers, and human beings are far too slow. All of this, and many other cognitive biases and shortcuts, contrive to make our minds progressively more exposed.

Technological advances, be they the invention of gunpowder or the development of satellites, have always brought changes in military organization and doctrine. Some technologies, such as the internet or satellite positioning (GPS), were first developed for military purposes before seeping into everyday use.

The US military has been working on cognitive warfare for a long time. So have the Russians and the Chinese, who have developed specific doctrines. I draw here on elements of the aforementioned report compiled for NATO by François du Cluzel.

Russia's use of asymmetric algorithmic warfare is well documented. We know that it has generated electoral interference in the West through the dissemination of false, misleading, and divisive information on social media, and we know how it has created troll factories and launched cyberattacks. All of this exploits the open nature of Western societies and their political and media ecosystems. The Russian approach builds on techniques and methods developed earlier by the Soviet Union. But the goal is no longer to convince anyone of the superiority of their system. "Rather, it is to sow doubt and distrust in order to undermine the enemy's system from within," explains Jean-Marc Rickli. "This approach, known as the doctrine of reflexive control, aims to pressure adversaries to act in Russia's interest by changing their perception of the world, with the secondary objective that the target is convinced that they are acting independently."

China, as is well known, operates on longer strategic planning horizons than Western countries. It has an explicit policy of dual civilian and military use of technologies. Its cognitive operations are organized around two axes. What they call fundamental cognition encompasses approaches and technologies that affect an individual's ability to reflect and function, while subliminal cognition focuses on emotions, willpower, and beliefs.

With the assistance of Rickli, and based on an essay[65] published by researchers with links to the Chinese military, let's try to better understand how an influence operation would unfold. "There are four phases. The first, which they call information disruption, is somewhat similar to what the Russians do at the level of reflexive control, which is to inject information or narratives, through state or recognized media, in order to influence the terms of the discussion," Rickli explains. He continues:

> The second phase, known as discursive competition, is based on what Daniel Kahneman describes in his book *Thinking, Fast and Slow*.[66] We have two systems of thought: System 1, instantaneous, intuitive, emotional, relying on impulses and biases, and System 2, much slower, rational, which aims to control System 1. Discursive competition targets our System 1, feeding existing biases or creating new ones, in order to foster the development of an information bubble.

The very nature of an information bubble is that it is very difficult to escape, to take into account information that contradicts or nuances what we have already come to believe.

> The third phase, the public opinion blackout, uses sentiment analysis to map a population, individual by individual, identifying each person's opinions and sensitivities, and then sending them targeted information at scale, primarily through social media. A sort of cognitive swarm, capable of generating a situation of confusion and chaos. This is completely new compared to what we've seen in the past. In disinformation or psychological warfare, you sent undifferentiated messages to an entire population, hoping to find an echo in some part of it. Today, you can target people precisely, with messages designed to resonate individually in order to orient their reactions according to specific objectives.

By definition, these operations are invisible, and can unfold even in peacetime. Only the fourth phase bears any resemblance to conventional warfare: "This would be the stage where an attempt is made to limit or cancel the adversary's ability to react, notably by neutralizing their infrastructures and communication systems." For example, with cyberattacks on digital systems or power plants and grids, or by bombing data centers.

Jean-Marc Rickli frames all this in terms of subversion. Democratic states are more susceptible to subversion attempts, "because they are characterized by open access to citizens, which is not the case in authoritarian states," he explains. This asymmetry means that "conducting counter-subversion operations is much more difficult for a democracy than for an authoritarian regime." Reacting to cognitive warfare attacks "requires a multifactorial response, across the entire social, civilian, and military spectrum—although predominantly nonmilitary. The first line of defense against this type of attack is therefore to increase the resilience of the population and of individuals."

In other words, protecting a form of cognitive autonomy is less a question of controlling information and more a matter of awareness of the threat, and of the collective will of democratic societies to remain so.

Faced with a rapid realignment of global power, European countries are currently pursuing ambitious security policies. After years of "peace dividends" and naïve and complacent attitudes, they are rethinking arrangements that have become wholly inadequate. Given what we have discussed so far, and given that most of the known cognitive campaigns convey antidemocratic views, it would seem necessary for new defense budgets, broadly construed, to include a substantial chapter dedicated to cognitive threats.

A first step is the establishment of early-warning monitoring and alert systems. France, for example, set up in 2021 a service responsible for vigilance and protection against foreign digital interference, called VIGINUM. Its mandate is to "preserve public debate from information manipulation coming from abroad on digital platforms."[67] Other countries have embarked on similar initiatives. As Jean-Marc Rickli explains, "Sweden established a psychological defense agency in 2022, especially in response to the war in Ukraine, since the Nordic countries are on the front line when it comes to Russian influence." This is not entirely without precedent. "Countries such as Sweden, Finland, and even Switzerland, with its comprehensive defense framework (*Gesamtverteidigung*), have already integrated during the Cold War this notion of resilience and psychological defense of the population." What is new are the technological means that allow cognitive warfare to be waged on a far larger scale, at low cost, rapidly, and in a targeted manner.

Part I / The algorithmic threat

12. Hypnocracy

In January 2025, a slim book by a young Hong Kong Chinese philosopher named Jianwei Xun was published in Italy. It was his first translation into a foreign language.

The book immediately garnered a great deal of attention: newspapers, television, references in conversations online and off. It evidently touched a nerve. Our society is drowning in an overproduction of reality. Digital technologies, in particular social media and artificial intelligence, increasingly define our relationship to the world and to each other, and influence political and economic priorities. Some of their codes are fairly explicit, such as the goal of making us tech-dependent. Others are less conspicuous, like algorithmic manipulation. Companies and politicians exploit and abuse this dynamic, assisted in the shadows by those whom writer Giuliano da Empoli calls the "engineers of chaos."[68]

In this blur of reality, where politics is becoming indistinguishable from an Instagram story, the right words can act as a lighthouse in the storm. And Jianwei Xun found one of those words. His book is entitled *Hypnocracy*.[69]

In it, he describes the "new regime of reality"[70] in which we live. A system in which power doesn't operates by means of force or rational persuasion, but through the algorithmic modulation of collective states of consciousness. Digital platforms and chatbots, Xun argues, reveal what they really are: not communication tools, but hypnotic systems that make up an architecture of suggestion and actively remodel the way we perceive and interpret reality:

> Hypnocracy is the first regime to act directly on consciousness. It does not control bodies. It does not repress thoughts. Rather, it induces a state of permanent trance. A lucid sleep. A functional trance. Wakefulness has been replaced by guided dream. Reality by continuous suggestion. With the submersion of the senses by constant stimuli, critical thinking is gently put to sleep and perception is reshaped, layer by layer. Meanwhile, screens shine incessantly in the night of reason.

While not entirely new (it updates for the algorithmic era some of the theses advanced sixty years ago by the French philosopher Guy Debord in *The Society of the Spectacle*[71]), the idea of hypnocracy is radical and uncomfortable. But given the shortage of concepts that can help us to give structure to our disorienting contemporary experience, it offers a powerful framework. It accounts simultaneously for the algorithmic manipulation of perception and for the political manipulation of attention, like that operated, for example, by US president Donald Trump, with his endless stream of announcements, provocations, memes, and outrages. It also helps to explain why rational responses gain so little traction: "While most analysts still focus on phenomena such as 'fake news' or 'post-truth,' what we are witnessing in Washington is a far more profound transformation: the emergence of a system where control is exercised not by suppressing the truth, but by multiplying narratives so that it becomes impossible to establish any fixed points of reference." A system where the intertwining and collision of the real and the unreal is constant and the intrusion of algorithms in our life is ultimately accepted without too much concern for its consequences.

Images of Trump dressed as the pope or as a king or as Jesus; Elon Musk's right arm raised in what may or may not be a Nazi salute; the president pouring excrement from an airplane over a group of protesting citizens; the brutal theatricality of immigrant deportations; the threats and blackmail aimed at countries that were once allies; the glaring lies: every provocation functions as what Xun calls a reality splitter, shattering shared context, creating parallel interpretative universes, and placing observers into distinct and irreconcilable information bubbles, according to their preexisting beliefs. As Xun argues:

> While critics continue to put forward rational arguments, statistics, and logical reasoning, they entirely fail to grasp that contemporary power now operates exclusively through the modulation of states of consciousness. Their critique remains trapped in the communication model of the Enlightenment, where truth must triumph on its own merits, without understanding that it is now an aesthetic product, a collective experience generated by repetition, by emotions, and by the suggestions of an algorithmic reality.

Just a few weeks later, as the book *Hypnocracy* continued to be discussed and commentated on, and was about to appear in French and other languages, it emerged[72] that the young Chinese intellectual did not actually exist. The book was itself a kind of aesthetic product, a narrative performance conceived by the Italian publisher and philosopher Andrea Colamedici. He wrote it in collaboration with two generative AI models, those of OpenAI and Anthropic, with which he is greatly familiar. His other job, indeed, is teaching *prompt thinking*—the subtle art of interrogating and dialoguing with AIs in order to obtain the desired results—at the European Institute of Design in Rome.

By injecting a captivating idea, albeit of artificial origin, into the cultural debate, Colamedici managed both to make his argument and to demonstrate it. Besides, while the Chinese philosopher is fictitious, the concept of hypnocracy is no less pertinent for it. It doesn't explain everything, yet it helps to understand a great deal of what concerns us here.

How, then, from within this dazed state, can we find the clarity of mind to confront the algorithmic influence over our minds? And, conversely, overwhelmed by technological acceleration, how do we resist hypnocracy?

Part II
A short resistance handbook

Part II / A short resistance handbook

13. Creating laws and rules

When we are collectively confronted with a transformation of great magnitude and speed, the initial temptation is often to impose rules. To respond with laws. Setting limits and legally defining what is and isn't acceptable. Banning methods or products deemed harmful. Creating safeguards, rights, and obligations. Curbing the excessive accumulation of power.

It's a complicated matter. The mere mention of the words *regulation* and *ban* is often enough to provoke rejection. This is particularly true when the subject is technology. In recent years, strongly encouraged by the companies that produce it, the dominant narrative has become that regulation stifles technological innovation, slowing collective progress towards a radiant future. According to this somewhat absurdist reading, for example, protecting individuals from the extraction and abuse of their personal data or from the harmful effects of addictive systems might hobble the development of artificial intelligence.

Moreover, the absence of formal regulation imposed and enforced by a government does not imply a lack of rules. Instead, it means that the governing principles are those set by tech companies themselves—embedded in their software architecture and interface design ("code is law," as we saw in the first chapter) or written into their user agreements.

One possible response to the cognitive threat is therefore legal and regulatory. There are others, particularly social and cultural ones, which we shall come to. But let us begin with the law.

For a long time, the workings of the human mind were considered not just incomprehensible, but also inviolable. This is why the legal instruments that protect our freedoms generally do not account for the cognitive sphere. However, this inviolability is now being challenged by the convergence of two technologies: artificial intelligence, which can identify patterns in our personal data, and neurotechnology, which can decode our emotions and is beginning to pierce our thoughts. This leaves us open to a vertiginous challenge which, as things stand, is not reflected in the world's existing legislative corpus, nor in any international treaty.

There are agreements, declarations, and recommendations geared specifically to regulating neurotechnology. However, from a legal point of view, all are nonbinding.

Further, there are instruments containing dispositions or principles relevant to our theme. Freedom of thought is protected by Article 18 of the 1948 Universal Declaration of Human Rights, by Article 9 of the 1950 European Convention on Human Rights, and by Article 18 of the 1966 International Covenant on Civil and Political Rights. In principle, this means that an individual's freedom of thought can never be violated. In all three charters, however, it is associated with freedom of religion and conscience, while cognitive integrity is neither mentioned nor implied.

The European Union's frameworks on digital technology are probably the most ambitious and consequential. The 2016 General Data Protection Regulation (GDPR) sets out rules for the collection, processing, and storage of personal data. It also confers on individuals rights of control over how their information is used, such as the rights of access, rectification, and erasure (the latter is known as the "right to be forgotten"). The 2022 Digital Services Act contains consumer protection measures, notably on freedom of expression and data privacy. It also places greater responsibility on digital platforms for the information they disseminate. But while the principles they contain may be indirectly linked to it, neither of these two texts specifically addresses the risks of harm to cognitive integrity.

We come closer to our subject with the Artificial Intelligence Act (the AI Act) enacted by the European Union in 2024 and set to come into force in phases. This regulation has not pleased the big tech companies, who have been lobbying to weaken or delay it, with the active support of the Trump administration (and with some success). It governs the development, marketing, and use of AI systems through a risk-based approach, classifying them into four groups according to their potential impact.

Some applications are considered to be "minimal or no risk" and are therefore not regulated. Those deemed "limited risk" are subject, among other things, to transparency obligations. The main goal is to ensure, for example, that users are not deceived by chatbots pretending to be humans and that artificially generated information is clearly labeled as such. The third category is that of systems judged to be "high risk," which are therefore regulated. These include those used in critical infrastructures (water, electricity, healthcare) and those that could lead to prejudicial treatments of people. This group encompasses, for example, tools that sort CVs for recruitment, determine access to education or grade exams, or assess creditworthiness in loan applications. These systems must be rigorously tested before going to market and must be accompanied, throughout their use, by human supervision.

Finally, there are practices posing risks deemed to be "unacceptable" and which are therefore prohibited. These include, for example, social notation systems (which assign scores or ratings to citizens based on their behavior, online activities, or compliance with social norms, affecting their access to services or opportunities), predictive policing, and the use of real-time remote identification systems, such as face recognition, in public spaces. It is in this category, of unacceptable risks, that legislators have chosen to include cognitive threats and behavioral manipulation.

Here is an extract from Article 5.1.a of the AI Act:

> The following AI practices shall be prohibited [...] the placing on the market, the putting into service or the use of an AI system that deploys subliminal techniques beyond a person's consciousness or purposefully manipulative or deceptive techniques, with the objective, or the effect of materially distorting the behaviour of a person or a group of persons by appreciably impairing their ability to make an informed decision, thereby causing them to take a decision that they would not have otherwise taken.[73]

Other points in Article 5 forbid, for instance, the use of AI to infer the emotions of an individual in the workplace or at school. Neurotechnology, however, is not covered by this law.

In October 2025, Italy became the first European Union country to adopt a national legal framework compliant with the AI Act.[74]

Across the Atlantic, the United States does not seem to be in any hurry to regulate these tech developments. President Joe Biden signed an executive order in October 2023 for the "Safe, Secure, and Trustworthy Development and Use of AI."[75] It contained measures for national security, privacy protection, systems reliability, and prevention against discriminatory bias. It was a cautious first step which was also part of a series of consultations with other countries on international AI governance, while placing considerable faith in industry self-regulation via voluntary codes of conduct.

The order lasted fifteen months. On January 20, 2025, just hours after being sworn in as president surrounded by the billionaire executives of big tech companies, Donald Trump revoked it. It hindered innovation in AI, he claimed, thus asserting the primacy of competitiveness and economic interests over the protection of citizens. The decision can be explained by geostrategic, industrial, and cultural reasons. But the result, in the words of AI pioneer Yoshua Bengio on stage at a TED conference, is that in the United States today "a sandwich has more regulation than AI."[76]

Five months later, three American senators introduced a bill on the Management of Individuals' Neural Data (which gives the fitting acronym MIND). But the proposal merely instructs a government commission to study how neural data should be protected.[77]

To find the first Constitution that explicitly protects mental integrity, we have to look south. In 2021, Chile added the following paragraph to Article 19 of its Constitution:[78] "The scientific and technological development will be at the service [of individuals] and will be carried out with respect for life and physical and psychological integrity. The law [...] especially safeguards brain activity, as well as the information derived from it." In other words, mental integrity is a fundamental right and any technological development relating to it must be authorized by law.

That Chile was the first country to protect mental integrity does not seem accidental. In the early Seventies, under the presidency of Salvador Allende, the government began to experiment with technology-assisted political governance. The project called Cybersyn[79] aimed to develop a "cybernetic socialism." It never got to run its full course: in September 1973, Allende was killed in a coup led by Augusto Pinochet, and Cybersyn was abandoned. The Constitution amended in 2021 was still the one put in place by the dictator.

Discussions are underway in other Latin American countries on legislation along similar lines, such as Mexico (with a proposal clearly inspired by Chile), Brazil, and Argentina. In 2022, the Latin American and Caribbean Parliament, an organization promoting regional integration and known as Parlatino, established a Model Law[80] on neurorights. Translated and summarized, the main safeguards that it contains are:

> The right to mental privacy, and the inalienable right not to be subjected to any form of intervention on one's neuronal connections, interference with cognitive processes, or intrusion into the brain through the use of neurotechnology, brain-computer interfaces, or any other system or device, without free, explicit, and informed consent, and even in cases where such intervention could be carried out unconsciously.

Parlatino's work echoes that of the Neurorights Foundation,[81] a group of scientists, ethicists, and technologists who originated the concept of neurorights. It describes the human rights protections needed to meet the challenges posed by the development of neurotechnology. There are five core neurorights. First: the right to mental privacy, or the ability to protect one's mental activity against any sort of disclosure. Second: the right to identity, or the ability to control one's mental integrity and identity. Third: the right to free will, that is, freedom of thought and natural agency and the freedom to choose one's actions. Fourth: the right to augmentation, or the guarantee of equitable access to improvements in cognitive abilities made possible by technology. Fifth: the right to protection, that is, against algorithmic bias.

Switzerland is another country in which a legislative framework is being discussed. In late 2024, an initiative was submitted to parliament to amend Article 10 of the Federal Constitution.[82] Currently, amongst other things, it stipulates: "Every person has the right to personal liberty and in particular to physical and mental integrity." The initiative aims to explicitly add the protection of cognitive integrity.

"If our ancestors didn't enshrine cognitive integrity in the Constitution alongside physical and mental integrity," Isabelle Chappuis, centrist MP and promoter of the initiative, told me,

> it is simply because they could never have imagined that our minds would become a target. Today, they are, and we therefore need to protect them. By anchoring this right in the Constitution, we would place it above freedom of trade and market logic. It would become, in effect, a sort of compass for legislating on AI, algorithms, and on technologies yet to come.

Chappuis is arguing here not only for a constitutional amendment but for a fundamental reorientation. In many countries, the choice of prioritizing commerce and trade has often led to the criticism, watering-down, or abandonment of many regulatory attempts in various areas. But in the face of the cognitive threat, she says, it is imperative to prioritize our right to think freely, our cognitive sovereignty over economic motives. In doing so, we would draw a boundary, both symbolic and legal, that could become the structuring axis of the ethics and regulation of tomorrow's technologies. It is worth underscoring that this is the opposite of the stance taken by Donald Trump which we described a few paragraphs earlier.

To close this short catalogue of attempts at regulation (which is representative but by no means exhaustive), it should be mentioned that, in September 2024, California, home to many of the major technology companies, became the first American state to introduce the protection of "brain data" into law.[83]

Finally, the work of two technology ethicists: Marcello Ienca of the EPFL in Lausanne and the Technical University of Munich and Roberto Andorno of the University of Zurich. They propose[84] four new human rights to protect what they call "the last refuge of personal freedom and self-determination": our minds. We have already encountered the first three: the rights to cognitive freedom, mental integrity, and mental privacy. The fourth is the right to psychological continuity. This concept refers to each person's ability to maintain the perception of their own identity, the consistency and stability of their psychological experience over time. To perceive themselves "as persisting through time as the same person."

Let's consider that last sentence again: the ability to perceive ourselves as a persistent entity. The purpose of this proposed right is to anticipate a future in which neuroscience, AI, and other technologies could interfere with our cognition to the point where we are no longer able to perceive ourselves over time as the same person. To the point where we, quite literally, lose our minds.

Philosopher Mark Hunyadi, from the University of Louvain in Belgium, thinks that this is still insufficient. "AI is a technology of the mind, a technology of our relationship to the world," he says: "Never before has technology, in all its known forms, exerted such a strong influence on the social and individual organization of humankind. Technology was man's aid; it has become his condition." To frame its future trajectory, to make sure that we move towards "a harmonious coexistence between human intelligence and the technologies it has created," Hunyadi believes that we need a new normative arrangement, set at a higher level: a standard for the sovereignty of the mind. A marker, he says, historically comparable in significance to human rights during the industrial revolution.

He has proposed[85] a Universal Declaration of the Rights of the Human Mind. Its eight articles include a provision that "The human mind must be protected, in particular, from all harmful intrusion, including that resulting from digital technologies, in order to guarantee its mental privacy, the source of all genuinely human achievements." Another article calls for the establishment of an international authority dedicated to the protection of the human mind. This initiative is now championed by the movement Rise for the Mind.[86]

The role of the declaration and of the authority, Hunyadi adds, "would not be to solve the problems, but to set the framework within which the problems can be solved."

Developing legal and regulatory tools in a domain advancing as rapidly as algorithmic technologies is, as we've just seen, an enormously complex undertaking. On one side, it is essential to reconcile the protection of fundamental values and principles, such as human rights, with the flexibility needed not to stifle innovation. On the other, it is necessary to define clearly the responsibilities of the companies that design and use tools capable of influencing or altering not only political and social dynamics, but cognitive processes themselves.

The right balance will also need to be struck between the right of individuals to the protection of their private cognitive spheres and the collective interest. This might in some cases require permitting a limited and proportionate incursion into mental intimacy—for example, to monitor a train driver's alertness levels through sensors. It's a thorny discussion: how far can we legitimately influence or monitor cognitive processes without encroaching on fundamental freedoms?

Is there a level of cognitive influence that might be broadly considered acceptable?

Furthermore, if we don't fully understand how artificial intelligence works and why it produces certain results, what level of autonomy should we grant to these systems? To what extent should an AI be permitted to determine for itself what it can decide on? If synthetic entities, with cognitive capabilities that imitate our own, start sharing our lives, what rights and responsibilities should be imputed to them? Will we have to grant them legal personality? Or psychological protections? Who owns the data generated by our interactions with chatbots? If people entrust them with information about their health, their emotional states, or their personal difficulties, should a professional confidentiality obligation apply to machines? A kind of client–attorney privilege? A Hippocratic oath designed for AI? Or an obligation to report suicidal or homicidal tendencies expressed by a user?

These are just some of the enormous ethical and regulatory questions raised by the rapid advance of artificial intelligence and neurotechnology.

But let's return to the sphere of cognitive warfare, where attacking our minds serves a strategy of conquest. A brief reminder, in the form of a question: what is won in cognitive warfare? Isabelle Chappuis: "Minds are won, and therefore decisions are won. Whoever masters cognitive warfare doesn't need to occupy a territory: they occupy brains. They sow doubt, divide, distract attention, and weaken the collective will. In the end, the other side collapses on its own, without even realizing it."

The use of cognitive technology and methods for military ends raises, among other things, the question of international law and its relevance to this context. Algorithmic and neurocognitive weapons, as we have seen, are currently subject to no international agreement. By contrast, there are conventions on chemical and biological weapons, and treaties against nuclear proliferation. This begs the question of whether, in the current scenario of rapid geostrategic realignment and economic and military competition, it is realistic to think of new international rules on cognitive warfare. "It's certainly not realistic right now. But I believe they are indispensable. It's a bit like the rules on chemical or nuclear weapons. Treaties send a strong normative signal. Even if someone cheats, and as we know this happens often, the rule at least draws a kind of moral boundary. It says what is intolerable and fixes red lines," says Isabelle Chappuis.

Algorithmic subversion is becoming a key feature of global power and influence strategies, adds Jean-Marc Rickli. He believes it would be appropriate to create a "regime on subversion control, mimicking those on arms control." The exponential growth of cognitive interference and AI-assisted disinformation, he says, "has created a new class of WMD: not weapons of mass destruction, but weapons of mass disinformation. Which could ultimately be transformed into weapons of mental destruction."[87]

Unlike nuclear weapons, whose development and management are controlled by states, algorithmic technologies are driven by the private sector, whose objectives are primarily commercial. Given the size and reach (and technological grip over our lives) of the big tech companies, however, their activities have serious political impacts. Furthermore, a treaty may contain the proliferation of nuclear weapons, but, as Rickli says, the fluid, open, and interconnected nature of the digital space "makes it impossible to stop the proliferation of lines of computer code." They can be copied and replicated fast, invisibly, and irretrievably. He flags up the danger of malicious actors, regardless of whether they are states or independent groups, exploiting AI to create far-reaching disruption. "This makes the creation of national and international technological governance structures even more essential."

Laws, rules, and governance structures are fundamental, but they cannot face alone the dynamism of technological evolution. Society as a whole must be made more robust, and the individuals who compose it must be prepared. Because there is something that we have somewhat forgotten, especially in Europe, although one only needs to think of the events of recent years in Ukraine to realize it: while it is the military that leads the battles, it is entire countries that fight—or defend themselves—in wars.

In a data-centered era, it is primarily through digital intermediaries that we decode the world, that we debate it and decide how to act within it. Our public and political spaces, as well as our individual and collective imaginations, are increasingly defined by digital, algorithmic technologies.

In response, the concept of "digital sovereignty" has gained traction in the European political debate: a country's ability to protect its information, its technological infrastructures, and, above all, the integrity of its public conversation and its economic system, and to act autonomously within its own digital space.

Digital sovereignty now determines its political counterpart, defined by the Merriam-Webster dictionary as "freedom from external control."[88] Europe's digital sovereignty is severely limited. A handful of American tech companies control most of the data centres, undersea cables, and satellites that make up the world's digital infrastructure; they control the "social" and AI platforms that constitute its informational architecture; and they control the operating systems of smartphones, which are the gateways to the intimate lives of users. European businesses and banks, hospitals and research labs, energy systems and governments themselves run on the servers and software of American multinationals.

For decades, European countries accommodated this, as did the other allies of the United States. The American government's commitment to a stable, predictable, rules-based, multilateral international order, however unevenly applied, seemed broadly solid and lasting. The rapid transition towards a world based on power and force, together with the questioning of historical alliances, often replaced by openly hostile postures and brazen interferences, is now transforming American technological domination into a primary source of systemic vulnerability for European countries. In the words of the Merriam-Webster editors, the European states are not free from external control.

This reasoning applies beyond digital technology. The global financial system, dominated by the dollar; advanced "integrated" weapons systems; as well as minerals and energy—all are major factors of dependence and loss of sovereignty.

If there is one image that should have awakened Europeans from their torpor, from the naïve belief that big tech companies are simply commercial enterprises that sell services, and that laws and contracts suffice for everything to go well, if there is one such image, it is a photograph that made the rounds of the world on January 20, 2025. On that day, lined up behind Donald Trump during his inauguration as President of the United States, there were none of his incoming government ministers. They were relegated to the third row. Just behind Trump were the multibillionaire bosses of American tech. The heads of Amazon, Apple, Google, Meta, X, and others. Companies that are themselves quasi-states, whose boards of directors and CEOs make decisions that have systemic and individual consequences for billions of people.

That image signaled Big Tech's conversion from an economic project into a political movement and its alignment with the Trump administration's priorities. It revealed the convergence of political power and "cloud power." It "sent a clear signal to the world: Technology is going to play a central role in the new administration's disruption of the global order," Robert Muggah, security expert and cofounder of the Brazilian think tank Igarapé, and Misha Glenny, rector of the Institute for Human Science (IWM) in Vienna, wrote in an article published in *Foreign Policy* magazine.[89]

"Silicon Valley's role is fundamentally changing, as well: It is quickly turning into an instrument of US coercion," a vector of the global projection of America's power, as manifest as military alliances and the dollar. The authors cite, amongst other things, the case of the war in Ukraine: "Even before Trump's election victory last November [2024], Elon Musk was conducting his own private foreign policy by restricting Ukrainian forces' access to Starlink in Russian-occupied Crimea. [...] In February, Musk publicly flirted with the idea of 'shutting down' the more than 15,000 Starlink terminals underpinning Ukraine's battlefield communications." According to a more recent Reuters investigation,[90] Musk did exactly that at least once, in late 2022, when Ukraine was trying to retake territory in the region of Kherson, codetermining therefore the outcome of that battle.

Starlink is, of course, the satellite service controlled by SpaceX, the space venture owned by Elon Musk, one of the richest men in the world. It provides internet connections through a constellation of thousands of satellites in low orbit around the Earth. It has around 7 million clients, a third of which are in the United States. In parts of the world where populations have no—or only limited and unstable—access, such as Mali, northern Kenya, or Sudan, Starlink terminals are literally a gift from the sky. I have used them myself on trips to remote areas. However, the company exists in symbiosis with the American government and, therefore, from the standpoint of international security, it represents for other countries another vector of dependency and erosion of sovereignty. Furthermore, the fact that an extremely wealthy and brilliant, yet unstable, capricious, and hubristic individual can wield the kind of personal influence described by Muggah and Glenny, and by Reuters, and hold such leverage over political and military leaders, is itself a significant risk multiplier. In this context, reports that some European governments, such as Italy, are considering entrusting their strategic communications to Starlink should provoke serious concern.

Many policymakers still appear not to have grasped that over the past twenty or so years these technologies have mutated. They are no longer products, that one buys and then owns. They have become platforms, architectures within which we live and work, and do so following the rules established by their owners. Think of software. In a past that already seems remote, you bought a spreadsheet or a graphics program, installed it, and used it on your computer. There is now barely any significant software that doesn't operate "in the cloud," with data and processing hosted and executed on remote servers, controlled, together with updates, changes, and above all access authorizations, by the companies that produce them rather than locally by the user.

This reasoning can be applied to any digitally connected system. Several European countries are, for example, buying or considering buying American F-35 fighter jets. Calling them airplanes is reductive. They are better understood as the focal point of a complex network of information flows, satellites, navigation and targeting aids, weapons and spare parts, proprietary computer code, sensors and integrated data, global logistics, maintenance and upgrades (and now also AI-based "aerial battle management solutions"[91]) all of which depend, to remain operational, on the goodwill of the American government. In the jargon, this is called strategic enablement: habilitation through shared technological architecture.

Even electric and self-driving cars, hospital and healthcare management systems such as Epic, and of course artificial intelligence, are no longer products: they are platforms. Optimized and highly performing. But implying dependence and subordination. And "dependence can be turned into a political weapon," as Marietje Schaake, a former member of the European Parliament now at Stanford University's Cyber Policy Center, wrote in the *Financial Times*.[92] "Will the world realize that adopting American AI will give an even more effective tool for coercion," she asks.

Another way to frame the issue is this: we are accustomed to considering the more than 700 military bases, large and small, controlled by the United States on every continent (including dozens each in Italy, in Germany, and in the United Kingdom) a physical expression of the projection of American power across the world. Given the centrality of digital infrastructure to the functioning of modern societies, however, it would now be entirely appropriate to also consider every data center of a US company, which is subject to American law wherever in the world it happens to be located, as a form of strategic presence akin to a military base.

The American government doesn't even try to disguise this. In July 2025, Donald Trump announced his artificial intelligence action plan:[93] in summary, acceleration, facilitation, priority to infrastructures, no taxes, and no regulations. The document is titled *Winning the Race* and starts with these words: "It is a national security imperative for the United States to achieve and maintain unquestioned global technological dominance." One of the tools for achieving this goal of unchallenged domination is economic blackmail. "Countries that attack our incredible American Tech Companies" with "Digital Taxes, Legislation, Rules, or Regulations" will be subject to "substantial additional Tariffs" and restricted access, for example to American semiconductors, Trump wrote.[94] Without explicitly mentioning the European Union, but directly targeting it and trampling on its sovereignty, as well as its laws (which apply to all companies, not just American ones). His Secretary of State Marco Rubio echoed him when commenting, at the end of 2025, on a 120 million euros fine levied by the EU on the X platform—for behavior contrary to European laws on European territory—in these terms: "it's an attack on all American tech platforms and the American people by foreign governments."[95] In other words, the interests of technology companies are assimilated to the interests of "the American people." A few days later, five Europeans—including former EU Commissioner Thierry Breton—were banned from entering the United States, with Rubio accusing them of wanting to "force American platforms to ban American views they oppose,"[96] a rhetorical sleight of hand that frames the legitimate regulation (in Europe, by Europeans) of markets as a conflict over free speech or censorship. When it is precisely the American government that is trying to impose on Europe its own framework (no rules, no taxes, no privacy protections) for technology.

We find ourselves, as the Dutch commentator Bert Hubert puts it,[97] "in the bizarre situation that anyone with any sense can see that America is no longer a reliable partner, and that the entire large-scale US business world bows to Trump's dictatorial will, but we still are doing everything we can to transfer entire governments and most of our own businesses to their clouds," to their digital infrastructure. This applies not only to complex, large-scale systems, but also to everyday practices including, for instance, the case of ministers of European countries exchanging sensitive information via WhatsApp, owned by Meta, one of the least trustworthy companies on the planet.[98] Not only "is it scary to have all your data available to US spying," adds Hubert, "it is also a huge risk for your business/government continuity. From now on, all our business processes can be brought to a halt with the push of a button in the US."

One button, perhaps not. But a sequence of buttons, following a political decision, probably. In practice, the US government "can exclude any European citizen from their own country's banking system and digital space," as Nicolas Guillou, a French judge at the International Criminal Court (ICC), has explained, and experienced.[99] Guillou presides over the chamber dealing with the situation in Palestine and is thus involved in the arrest warrant issued against Israeli Prime Minister Benjamin Netanyahu and others, a move that in 2025 earned him to be sanctioned by Donald Trump. Thousands of people worldwide are subject to American sanctions, mainly terrorists or alleged terrorists, members of criminal organizations, or political leaders. And now, also nine ICC judges (Guillou and colleagues), whose job is to uphold international law.

What does this mean in practice? The freezing of accounts with American companies like Airbnb or Amazon, the refusal of services by others, the blocking of package deliveries (if any American intermediary is involved), the inability to access e-mails and documents if they are hosted on US platforms, and, above all, the freezing of assets, the closure of bank accounts—even across the eurozone—and exclusion from payment methods (Visa and Mastercard are American, as are Apple Pay and PayPal). Any transaction with or via a US company, or where the central currency is the dollar (which is almost always the case outside Europe), becomes impossible. It's a bit like going back to living in the 1990s, Guillou observed with some irony, meaning without access to the digital infrastructure of contemporary daily life.

ICC members are not the only ones in this situation. Brazilian judge Alexandre de Moraes, who led the prosecution against former Brazilian president Jair Bolsonaro, has also been hit with similar sanctions. It is worth noting that, in both cases, these are political decisions (Bolsonaro and Netanyahu are aligned with Trump) taken in retaliation for the application of non-US laws in jurisdictions outside of the United States. But that hardly matters, because the pervasiveness of tech platforms and the fact that the US increasingly attributes extraterritorial character to its laws give the American government the power to exclude any unwanted organization or person from the digital space.

The Cloud Act,[100] for example, a law passed in 2018 during Trump's first presidency, requires (Section 2713) tech providers to "preserve, protect, or disclose [to the US government] the contents of any electronic communication, record, or other information concerning a customer or subscriber that is in the possession, custody, or control of such provider," regardless of whether such data "is located within or outside the United States."

16. De-Americanizing our tech

In a context where public debate happens largely in digital form, protecting political sovereignty requires preserving digital sovereignty. European countries will not be able to do so, nor to safeguard the cognitive integrity of their citizens, without de-Americanizing as much as possible their technological and information infrastructure.

It's one of those ideas that test the limits of our imagination: de-Americanizing ourselves. A bit like thinking of transcending the dogma of economic growth, or taxing the ultra-rich. We sigh "it's impossible" and go off to worry about something else.

For sure, renouncing American products would require us "to strip away a large part of our physical, mental, and symbolic universe," as the editor of the Swiss weekly *Azione*, Carlo Silini, put it.[101] America permeates not only our objects, but also our society and our minds, he suggests. By this he means, of course, technology, social media, smartphones and computers, entertainment platforms, video games, and the dominant AI chatbots. But also the films and series that pour the American way of thinking across our cinemas and television screens; the cartoons that shape still-developing brains; music and its aesthetic and social representations; the fantasies of the "frontier" and of the "land of the free"; internet memes; junk food; Halloween; celebrity worship; business management methods and commercial and financial practices; advertising and promotional messages. Without forgetting the omnipresence of the American political debate and social traits that, by mimicry, slowly infiltrate themselves and are reproduced in European discussions, imposing their themes, their spectacle, their (di)visions of the world, and their cultural civil war. In the words of the writer Christophe Gallaz, this results in a "collective mental bain-marie" in which we are immersed. De-Americanizing ourselves, and in particular resisting algorithmic control (we will focus on this here, even if the topic itself is much broader), will require, as Silini writes, a "painful jolt of pride and will."

To better understand the extent of this dependence, let us consider some data. A study by the company Proton (which sells alternative solutions to American ones, so these results should be interpreted with caution) analyzed the e-mail programs and the relative security systems employed by publicly listed European companies.[102] Since e-mail underpins most corporate digital systems, the authors estimate that many organizations using American messaging tools also "use other services such as cloud storage" from the same providers. The study's central finding was that more than 74 % of European listed companies depend on American technology. The most dependent countries are Iceland (97 %) and Norway (96 %), with Belgium at 80 %. Among the large countries, the least exposed is Germany (at 58 %, nonetheless). Italy is at 69 %, Switzerland at 68 %, France at 66 %. Eastern

European countries show higher levels of independence, but only just, such as Poland (45 %) and Slovakia (43 %). Each country has a different distribution of sectoral dependencies, but in general these figures confirm that, were access to American platforms suddenly restricted, due to a failure or intentionally, essential services—from electricity and water to healthcare, banks, and transport—and production and commercial activities could be significantly disrupted, or halted entirely.

Another report, carried out by the firm Asterès for a network of major French companies and public administrations (Cigref), estimated the economic impact of purchases of American cloud services and software by European companies (without taking computer equipment and other services into account).[103] The study, which took in only companies headquartered in the EU, excluding public administrations and private individuals, concluded that American suppliers control an 83 % share of the European market, representing a value of 264 billion euros. A figure comparable, in order of magnitude, to the total energy imports of the European Union (360 billion euros in 2024). The study also estimated the potential economic impact of redirecting these flows: "If 10 % of purchases of cloud / software services were redirected to European providers by 2030," it could result in "the creation of around 331,000 jobs," injecting new momentum into the entire European technology sector.

That figure of 264 billion euros per year refers, it's worth underscoring, only to purchases of American cloud services and software by companies based in the EU. If we add the spending of public administrations and private individuals on equivalent or other services, the purchases of digital equipment (including smartphones) and the outlays by European entities outside the EU (such as the Swiss or Norwegian governments and companies), we can estimate that the figure more than doubles. Let's put this in perspective. The so-called

Draghi Report,[104] the study by the working group chaired by the former president of the European Central Bank, Mario Draghi, on the continent's competitiveness, estimated in September 2024 that the European Union needed additional annual investments of around 750–800 billion euros. Just a little more, then, than the amount Europeans spend to buy digital services and equipment from US companies.

This does not yet account for the hundreds of billions invested directly by European funds of all kinds—from banks to venture capital to pension funds to sovereign wealth funds—in American tech companies. Just one example: as part of managing its foreign currency reserves, the Swiss National Bank holds investments[105] totaling over 170 billion dollars in hundreds of US companies. About 60 billion of that is invested in just nine[106] of the largest tech companies, the very ones we discuss in this book.

The problem is not only collective. A few weeks after reading Silini's article, I had coffee with a friend who lives in Scandinavia. Cosmopolitan and a polyglot, she works internationally. At one point she put down her cup, smiled, and remarked confidentially: "I bought a Samsung." By which she meant the smartphone placed on the table next to her, screen down. "I've always had iPhones, but I don't want an American phone anymore. And I don't want a Chinese one either." She is not naïve and knows full well that Samsung, a South Korean company, makes devices that work with an American operating system, Google's Android: "It's not ideal, I know, but I want less America in my life."[107]

Her words are easy to smile at: from the point of view of user capture, Google is no improvement on Apple, the maker of the iPhone. But they reflect the sentiment of a growing number of Europeans: the awareness that our lives depend on American technological systems, and that it has become a real problem.

This does not mean a desire to switch to the other global technological track, the Chinese. Nor to think of an autarkic approach. It expresses, rather, an aspiration to regain some level of control, a degree of emancipation, autonomy, choice.

It's a complex issue. Disconnecting from established digital infrastructures or developing alternatives is difficult and costly in both time and money. From a technical point of view, the entire technological ecosystem is made up of integrated and interlocking elements of varying origins: the machines that engrave chips are Dutch, the chips are *engineered* in the USA but *manufactured* in Taiwan, the software is American or European, the devices Chinese. In this context, digital sovereignty looks less like a binary option (sovereign/not sovereign) and more like a spectrum, a gradation.

Regardless of the difficulties, "everything that can be done, should be done," the Italian tech journalist Luca De Biase told me when I discussed this with him. I had contacted him after he published an essay[108] in the online magazine *Le Grand Continent* on the need for a "war of European digital independence."

His argument is that Europeans have come to accept the premise that the monopoly of American platforms is the legitimate result of their competitiveness, and that there is nothing concrete to be done against this power. Europe has allowed itself to be "cognitively colonized" by renouncing its digital independence, says De Biase. The time has come to reclaim it.

While it is theoretically possible "to intervene by law on the behavior of the existing platforms [...] their power is such that many of the measures decided in their regard prove entirely ineffective," he writes. Even more so when the American presidency itself threatens economic retaliation for any European regulation or taxation of technology companies. The best way to limit the power of big tech would therefore be to create alternative and superior platforms in Europe.

We've heard that before, some will say. It's true. Others will remember the failed attempts to create European competitors with public funding, such as the Quaero project ("I seek" in Latin), launched in 2005 by a group of governments, research institutions, and companies with the ambition of competing with Google (and, at the time, with Yahoo!). Cost: 200 million euros. The idea that great technological innovations can emerge in a "planned" way is generally considered aberrant in a context of liberal market economy, and rightly so.

But this is not what Luca De Biase is arguing. He is not proposing recreating American platforms, just more ethical ones, or injecting public money into technology startups. He points rather to the development—urgently and resolutely—of a European model that is not a copy of either the American or the Chinese approach. A new kind of industrial policy aimed at establishing the context and introducing logics of innovation that can nurture distinct approaches.

Let's mention some keywords: interoperability (the ability for users to move freely from one platform to another without losing functionality, data, or contacts, a bit like changing smartphones and operators without having to give up their phone number); the prohibition of recommendation algorithms (which are the central mechanism of addiction, disinformation, and polarization); transparency (for instance on the nature of the data on which AIs are "trained"); open-source software; as well as respect for essential European values such as human rights. Plus: business models that do not rely on the often abusive exploitation of personal data, but favor technology that does *not* spy on people. It's a partial list, but you'll notice that it describes what American platforms are not.

The aim, De Biase writes, should not be to build "a new big platform," but "a big number of new platforms" that are interoperable and transparent and that can work in a federated rather than centralized way. Laying the groundwork for "transforming a system monopolized by a few [American] giants into an open, competitive market rich in innovation," free and pluralistic, and in which "the excessive concentration of added value and power" is diluted.

One initiative moving in this direction is called EuroStack.[109] A technological stack (tech stack) is the set of tools, programming languages, and technologies used to build and run an application, a website, or a digital service. It can be imagined as a layered structure, in which each layer has a precise role (interface, security, database, storage, transactions, etc.) and the assembled whole forms the final system users interact with.

As the name EuroStack suggests, the initiative aims to reduce technological dependence by promoting the development of a European tech stack, from semiconductors to the cloud, right down to the software components, federating what already exists and mobilizing the necessary resources (hundreds of billions of euros). Launched in 2025, the project is supported by a wide range of stakeholders.

When Luca De Biase writes that Europeans seem to regard American platforms as inescapable, he echoes a widespread comment: the real challenge, we often hear, is the lack of European alternatives to the American technology giants.

The phrase is repeated like a mantra. The more it appears in consultants' reports, press articles, and political statements (since the time of Margaret Thatcher, but recently with increasing frequency, politics has made "there is no alternative," known as TINA, the excuse for a lot of things), the more it sounds true. But is it?

If you pay attention to the way the phrase "Europe lacks alternatives to the tech giants" is used, you may notice that the emphasis almost always falls on the word "giants." The implication being that, since Europe does not have a Google or an Amazon, then it has nothing. This assumes that there is only one way to develop technology, which is by aiming to operate on a super-sized scale, in a centralized way, and leaving a small number of companies in control.

While the absence of large European tech players is indeed a significant problem, it is interesting to note that the emphasis seldom falls on the word "alternatives." Almost nobody ever asks whether substitutes exist for the actual type of digital technologies and services that are needed. We are so fixated on the *big* in Big Tech that we forget the *tech*.

There's no doubt that Google is a unique search engine. That at the moment the scalability of the Microsoft cloud would be hard to match in Europe. That if we want to work on a laptop, it's almost impossible to avoid American (or Chinese) devices: there are niche Taiwanese and Japanese brands, but practically no European ones. And, of course, most smartphones run on American operating systems, iOS and Android, from Apple and Google, respectively. However, for a large number of technological needs, particularly in terms of software, viable alternatives do exist: operating systems, storage and cloud, productivity and office applications (including full alternatives to Microsoft365), data management, CRM, file transfer, secure messaging, meetings and video conferencing, scheduling, security, 3D graphics, VPNs, payment systems, and AI. Often the companies that supply them are national or transnational, not continental, and therefore "small." In terms of quality, though, they're often comparable to the big ones, and even when their performance is marginally lower, 10 percent less efficiency seems a reasonable price to pay for 100 percent more sovereignty and control. In some areas, such as industrial (automation) or sector-specific artificial intelligence, European companies are actually more advanced.

But instead of purchasing from national or European players, thus helping them grow, enrich their technological offer, retain and strengthen local talents and competencies, develop capabilities and assets, and contribute to the vitality of national and continental innovation ecosystems, most European decision-makers, whether business leaders or politicians, continue almost by default to fund the capture of European economies, governments, and minds by American Big Tech. Perhaps we need to also de-Americanize the way we look at our own reality.

One possible way to unlock this impasse is public procurement. The money that public administrations at all levels spend on buying digital technologies and services. In Europe, this amounts to many tens of billions of euros every year. Andy Yen, founder and CEO of the multinational Proton in Geneva, thinks that this leverage could be used to support European tech. "You can't dictate to a private company what tech it should buy," he told the Swiss newspaper *Le Temps*."[110] But "you can perfectly well decide how public money, that of European taxpayers, is spent. Europe does not suffer from a [technology] supply problem, but from a demand problem. Public demand has been captured by American and Chinese tech." Yen (along with many colleagues) is therefore calling for "a change of mindset in public sector investments and procurement policies: we should give priority to European businesses." Which is, after all, exactly what the Americans and the Chinese do with their own companies. Note that he's not talking about subsidies, but about bids, markets, purchases. Demand and supply.

Migrating to alternative platforms takes time, effort, reflection, an analysis of actual needs, well-thought-out strategies (and visionary specs for public procurement), and generates costs. It is simpler to "upgrade" with the same provider. This inertia explains, for example, why Microsoft, active in Europe since it launched its Word software in German and French about forty years ago, not only has a massive presence across European public administrations, at EU level as well as in individual countries, regions, and cities, but continues to extend it. Let's consider an example from my own country, Switzerland. In late 2024, the Swiss federal administration paid Microsoft 150 million francs for Office software licenses. The competent department explained that, "owing to interoperability and compatibility requirements, the deep integration of the existing system and the multiple interdependencies between specific applications, no alternative currently exists that would allow fault-free operation."[111] Translation: we are so captive that there is no alternative.

I single out Microsoft because it is a company that has for years, particularly through its very active "foreign minister," its president Brad Smith, assured anyone willing to listen of its "unwavering support" for Europe's digital infrastructure, its security and its resilience, "regardless of geopolitical and trade volatility."

In April 2025, on behalf of his company, Smith announced new "European digital commitments."[112] The following are some excerpts from the document (which is a dozen or so pages long):

> We respect European values, and adhere to European laws and actively defend Europe's cybersecurity. We recognize that European countries, like nations everywhere, need to have rock-solid confidence in the digital infrastructure on which they rely. We guarantee European customers the ability to have their data stored and processed in Europe. Our European datacenter operations and their boards will be overseen by a European board of directors that consists exclusively of European nationals and operates under European law. We will continue to protect the privacy of European data. We enable customers to control where their data is stored and processed, how it is encrypted and secured, and when Microsoft can access it. We back our technical solutions with strong contractual commitments.

Then, two months later, Anton Carniaux, head of corporate, external, and legal affairs at Microsoft France, was called to appear before the French Senate's committee of inquiry into public procurement.[113] Keep in mind section 2713 of the American Cloud Act from the end of the previous chapter. Question to Carniaux from Senator Dany Wattebled: "Can you guarantee before our committee, under oath, that the data of French citizens entrusted to Microsoft through UGAP [the French national public purchasing agency] will never be transmitted, following an order from the American government, without the explicit agreement of the French authorities?"

Carniaux's reply, under oath: "No, I cannot guarantee it."

Quite a few European public bodies have started to embrace alternative technologies. The Swiss Federal Tribunal (the country's Supreme Court of Justice) has opted to maintain control of its tech by using open source solutions. The French National Gendarmerie did the same.[114] Cities such as Lyon[115] in France and Copenhagen and Aarhus in Denmark have decided to dispense with Microsoft software and services, as has the German region of Schleswig-Holstein[116] (30,000 employees). Lyon's head of IT systems said that the change has also saved two-thirds of costs.[117] The two Danish cities must have inspired their national politicians, because the Minister for Digitalization, Caroline Stage, announced that her ministry would start migrating from Microsoft Office to LibreOffice.[118] The German government has put in place a policy framework for a German Tech Stack.[119] The French government has announced its intention to "reduce the state's extra-European digital dependencies." As the Minister of Public Action and Accounts, David Amiel, said: "We can no longer accept that our data, our infrastructure and our strategic decisions depend on solutions whose rules, prices, developments, and risks we do not control."[120]

And the International Criminal Court itself, following the exclusion of its magistrates from US platforms, decided[121] to replace Microsoft systems with the openDesk solution, developed by the Centre for Digital Sovereignty (Zentrum Digitale Souveränität[122]), a German para-public organization.

One could argue about which system offers the best features. But it is clear that, according to the analysis and experiences of these cities and governments, there is a panoply of non-US software able to meet their needs (as well as costing less). Above all, it does not pose a risk to national security. The Danish minister's decision was certainly encouraged by Donald Trump's repeated statements about the "strategic need" for the United States to seize Greenland, a Danish territory. Should real tensions arise between the two countries, dependence on American tech platforms would put Denmark in a rather precarious position.

David Monniaux of CNRS, the French national center for scientific research, sums up the issue with a not-so-far-fetched provocation published in *Le Monde*:

> One can perfectly well imagine the American president having a bout of ill-feeling towards France, perhaps on the grounds that it was obstructing his "peace plan" for Ukraine. From a geopolitical fiction perspective, what would happen if he ordered Big Tech to cease the cloud services provided to our government, our public administrations, our armed forces?[123]

Part II / A short resistance handbook

17. Recognizing manipulation

When Johannes Gutenberg began printing his first Bibles in Mainz, Germany, halfway through the fifteenth century, the Chinese had already been printing books for quite some time. Gutenberg's main innovation was the use of movable metal characters, individually cast, allowing texts to be composed more rapidly and easily. In other words, he invented a method for optimizing typography, accelerating the production of books, pamphlets, and religious documents while reducing costs. He also developed inks that were darker and more stable.

In so doing, he gave many more people the opportunity to express themselves, upending the social, religious, and political arrangements of the time. And triggering history's first information overload.

By the end of the fifteenth century, just fifty years after Gutenberg's first Bible, printing presses similar to his had spread to more than 110 European cities. In his essay *The*

History and Power of Writing,[124] the French historian Henri-Jean Martin estimates that readers at the time could already choose between 27,000 different printed titles, representing a total of 10 million copies in circulation across Europe. This, while there were only a few hundred thousand readers in a population of less than 100 million (Russia included).

According to Martin, the first printers modeled their books on the layout of manuscripts, striving to imitate the elegance of the scribes, to the point that two prayer books of the time "look like twins," he says, despite one being a medieval manuscript and the other a printed copy from 1472. Later, publishers and booksellers began to explore new formats, searching for a formal language and aesthetic better suited to printed books. In 1510 the first page numbering was introduced, based on Arabic numerals. Then came paragraphs, chapters, indexes, all tools designed to facilitate access to the information contained in the book. It was only towards the end of the sixteenth century, nearly 150 years after Gutenberg's invention, that books began to look like the ones we know today.

The response to that deluge of information was not, of course, limited to redesigning the physical book. It engaged the whole of society, over a very long period. With some audacity, one might argue that the school in its modern form, political parties, public administrations, courts of law, and, of course, the media—basically the entire infrastructure of modern society—are the result of the collective effort to organize, channel, filter, transmit, and render usable the ever-growing quantity of information unleashed by Gutenberg's invention.

The evolution of information technologies since Gutenberg has spawned many other profound social transformations. Let us consider an anecdote linked to the invention of the telegraph.[125] Historically, the maximum speed at which information could travel between two places had been that of a galloping horse or perhaps a carrier pigeon. Until the mid-nineteenth century, for example, there was no need to keep military operations secret. When a British warship set sail, the details of the mission were published in *The Times* of London. After all, there was no means by which the information could precede the ship to its destination.

Just a few years later, however, the telegraph network had extended right across Europe and would soon cross the oceans. The news from English newspapers could be rapidly transmitted all the way to India. For the first time in history, the speed of information became decoupled from that of its carrier. The telegraph radically transformed the art of war, espionage, trade (think of the possibility of arbitrage on the prices of goods), finance, administration, the news business, and, more generally, the value of information.

Then came the telephone, satellites, the internet, smartphones. And now, algorithmic technologies. Which don't ask for permission but simply seep into our lives uninvited (such as the AI integrated by manufacturers into the apps and software we use every day—we will return to this later). To all appearances, they land in a society that is not ready for them. Not culturally, not institutionally, not legally, not morally.

These technologies constitute a Gutenbergian challenge, a profound change in our relationship to information. A whole-of-society moment. And it is not necessary for AI to reach the "general" or "superintelligent" level, nor for it to be completely error-free, for it to be transformational. It already is. Its impacts are already tangible.

In a world where the fundamental stake is the control of cognitive capacities and of representations of reality, the most important resource a country possesses, its primary source of robustness,[126] consists of the educated minds of its citizens. Therefore, much in the future will be played out around these two words: educated and citizen. Both stand in direct opposition to the passivity of the consumer.

There are different ways of coping with the cognitive threat. For example, training citizens to be capable of recognizing manipulative narratives and, above all, algorithmic manipulation. For the moment, it feels as though we're navigating in the opposite direction. If we look, for instance, at education (but similar things could be said about work, or cultural production), since the invasion of everyday life by generative AI, a mixture of enthusiasm and disarray has been blowing through our schools and universities. Many students use AI to summarize books instead of reading them, or to generate essays that they will not learn to write and will be unable to explain, or as personal tutor or to offload homework. "Prompting" is certainly simpler and requires less commitment and responsibility than reading or writing. Homework is much easier with the help of ChatGPT. But if there's one thing school is supposed to teach, it is to develop intellectual curiosity and critical sense; and this means doing—and thinking—difficult things. "A student who cuts and pastes a history paper is enrolled in a cutting and pasting class, not a history class," says the media theorist and vice provost at New York University, Clay Shirky.[127]

The concern is that faking work (thanks to AI), rather than actually doing it, will genuinely stunt the development of skills and critical thinking. That the outsourcing of learning and reflection will generate a dependence on technology. That "there will be no more unassisted thought," as the cultural critic Tatjana Samopjan told me, "and that we will get used to being guided by something that has never had a real, embodied, and holistic experience of life."

This concern is not merely theoretical. Research takes time, but early indications, while confirming an increase in personal productivity, also suggest forms of de-skilling. A study conducted on a thousand students preparing for mathematics exams at high school, for example, showed that those with access to artificial intelligence scored notably better than those without.[128] Yet, when access was subsequently withdrawn, they performed significantly worse than the control group.

Many other studies have produced similar results. An MIT team asked participants in an experiment to write four essays over a period of four months with varying levels of technological assistance. Broadly speaking, they discovered[129] that the more help the subjects received, the less intense their brain activity was during the test, especially in the areas associated with cognitive processing, attention, and creativity. Which could translate, the researchers warn, into a "cognitive debt": the idea that the short-term gains in ease and productivity of using AI come at the price of a long-term deterioration in our ability to learn, remember, and think.

If we pay attention, we can notice the effects of this cognitive outsourcing in ourselves. The more digital technologies propagate in our lives, the more dependent on them we become and the harder it is to think and function without resorting to them. Those who, like me, are lucky enough to speak and write in several languages, for example, may have noticed an erosion of their linguistic elasticity, of their ability to easily switch from one language to another, or a shrinking repertoire of synonyms. In my case, as a freelance journalist, I would write an article in French and then open a new document on the other half of my screen and translate it on the fly, my eyes reading the French while my fingers typed the Italian or the English. A single proofreading was generally enough for the result to be ready for publication. Although I still use all my languages every day, I have lost some of that ability. I am slower. Words are no longer immediately accessible. Over the last few years, I have leant too heavily on machine translation systems such as Google Translate and DeepL (which are AIs), to which I have gradually transferred, in the name of speed and practicality, a portion of my faculties.

Another notable example of de-skilling concerns our ability to produce a mental map of the physical space and orient ourselves within it. The small blue GPS dot pulsing on our smartphone screens has replaced, for many people, the faculty of spatial orientation.

It is plausible that this gradual cognitive offloading could "lead to societies becoming more prosperous, more advanced, longer-lived [thanks to AI]—and less smart," writes the English education expert Daisy Christodoulou.[130] Drawing an analogy with obesogenic socioeconomic dynamics, Christodoulou evokes the danger of a "stupidogenic society," in which the systematic delegation of thinking to machines would threaten our ability to reason, just as ultra-processed foods and lack of physical activity alter our bodies.

A few studies do not represent the sum total of truth, of course, and the nuances of each one (the MIT study, which I have summarized above in a few lines, spans over 200 pages) do matter. But what we've seen so far prompts an interesting consideration. There is much debate around how AI will automate many jobs. A phrase that circulates widely on this subject, to the point of becoming a cliché, is that "it won't be AI that takes your job, but someone who uses AI." In light of the studies just cited, one might postulate the opposite: that people who preserve their cognitive capacities may be advantaged over those who become too dependent on the machines.

Let us digress briefly to speculate about how AI might really impact the world of work. We often hear that AI will lighten doctors' workloads and allow them to spend more time with patients, or that it will be applied to the tedious and repetitive tasks, freeing humans to concentrate on more complex or creative and rewarding activities. These scenarios are described by those who develop the technology and are therefore part of their marketing strategy. They are often reiterated by experts, which never fails to astonish me, since they reflect only a half-truth.

The "time saving" element is the part that is true. There is no doubt that AI systems will be capable, for example, of interpreting radiological images faster and cheaper than a doctor, or that the most automatable tasks of any job will be transferred to them. What will not materialize, or only marginally, is the part about AI enabling, say, more time to be spent with patients or being creative. Not because of technological limitations, but for economic reasons: nobody is going to pay for that.

If doctors do not currently devote enough time to patients, it is not for lack of AI. The healthcare sector is saturated with technology, yet many clinicians spend less and less time with patients. This is because the system in which they operate prioritizes performance, optimization, and speed (and, increasingly, profits) over humanity. It is most unlikely that, with the irruption of AI, most doctors will suddenly be encouraged to devote more (expensive) time to patients. Or, in a similar manner, that office workers will be free to spend time "creatively" while AI performs the work for which they are paid.

Of course, thanks to AI many things will take less time, or no time at all, and will be much easier and cheaper. Technology always transforms the sectors into which it is integrated. But it does not change their fundamental values and priorities. If the overriding value is profit and the priorities are to optimize, accelerate, and cut costs—to arbitrage on the cost of labor, above all—AI will be primarily used for that. Not to allow employees to do "more rewarding" things. But to replace them.

Faced with this risk, we often hear reassuring statements that, as with previous technological transitions, the jobs lost to AI will be offset by new opportunities. This historical consolation tends, however, to underestimate the radical novelty of AI, which we touched upon earlier: for the first time, we are faced with a technology that is not a simple tool, but a system that will be capable of autonomously making decisions that have direct effects on reality.

Schools and teachers (who also use AI to prepare lessons or mark students' work) have been caught off guard by the emergence of generative AI systems. It took a couple of years for guidelines and frameworks to begin to emerge. Curricula have been tweaked to include primarily an instrumental learning of the technology—how to use it—in order to train an AI-competent workforce. This is obviously very important, for there will be almost no profession, in the future, that will not have to interact with or collaborate with AI.

But being "educated" in the face of the cognitive threat means more than knowing how to use effectively the technologies that structure it. It means, above all, understanding how they are created and how they function. Learning to question their outputs, to identify their human, social, and ethical implications. And to decode the cultural, economic, and power structures within which these technologies exist and evolve.

Part II / A short resistance handbook

18. Loosening the digital grip

Perhaps it warrants to be said explicitly: the digital technologies we have discussed in this book, at the heart of which is artificial intelligence (which enhances and accelerates all the others), are not a passing phenomenon. They are becoming an invisible and inescapable infrastructure of our daily lives. An architecture that we inhabit. AI, in particular, however imperfect it currently is, promises real benefits, and we should do everything possible to exploit its positive potential in the best interest of the largest number of people.

Artificial intelligence is already integrated into many human, social, and economic processes. The media hype and financial exuberance surrounding it are certainly signs of an overestimation of its short-term impacts. A correction will be inevitable. But it would be dangerous to underestimate its long-term significance. Imagining that its advance could be halted, or that we might return to a world where these technologies are a domesticated and optional tool, is pure fiction.

As one of the main characters in Richard Powers' novel *Playground* says when talking to an AI: "The rest of human history, however short or long, will be spent hopelessly trying to contain you."[131]

On an individual level, the choice will not be ours for much longer. Artificial intelligence has long been deployed, for instance, in recommendation algorithms, the systems that suggest what to watch or buy, which guide our decisions while preserving the appearance that we are choosing freely. It is also being progressively integrated into the software that shapes our days, both privately and professionally. We use WhatsApp, Gmail and Apple Mail and up pops AI, uninvited. The same is true of Microsoft programs (one morning in late 2025, the members of the Swiss parliament discovered,[132] without having asked for it, that Microsoft had activated the AI "Copilot" functionality in their Office accounts), of Google searches, as well as of video conferencing applications. And above all of the operating systems of our phones, the most intimate machines of all. For the moment, it is still possible to decline the artificial "companions" proposed by Google on Android devices, by Apple on iPhones, and by Microsoft on Windows, while continuing to use these devices effectively. But that option will gradually disappear. The progressive integration of AI will make many functions dependent on this technology, and unusable without it. The (programmed) degradation of the usefulness of devices unless AI is activated will eventually force us into the inexorable embrace of the tech giants, with no possibility of opting out. Except, of course, if we stop using smartphones.

This scenario also foreshadows a new digital information ecosystem, whose supporting structure will no longer rest on websites but on the text or voice dialogue window with chatbots and agents. These will gradually become the universal interface between us and all information, connection, and transaction. The integration of AI-generated summaries at the top of Google search results, for example, has led to a drastic drop—of between two-thirds and three-quarters[133]—in clicks on links beneath them. Which suggests that users are generally inclined to accept the chatbots' answers as good enough.

It bears repeating that AI is trained on our data. Another way it insinuates itself into our lives uninvited is through the "right" that platforms and companies (Facebook, Instagram, WeTransfer, Zoom, Slack, Grammarly, Adobe, Amazon, to name but a few) arrogate to themselves to appropriate our private and professional information and documents to "improve the service," a euphemism that actually means to feed their artificial intelligence. If you store your photos or images on Microsoft's OneDrive, for example, the system "uses AI to recognize faces in your photos." In other words, it uses them to train its facial recognition tools. This is presented as a way to "help you find photos of friends and family."[134] Which in fact the machine does. And therein lies the real crux of this technology and our relationship with it: it offers real, practical, useful services, and makes us more effective. But at the price of data extraction, the erasure of privacy, and growing dependency. And all these companies make it deliberately very difficult to contest these practices.

Faced with the exponential progress of AI and its intrusion into our lives, some have concluded that it will soon overtake us: that we will be merely the *second* most intelligent species on Earth. And the hundreds of billions of dollars being invested in this technology worldwide are working precisely in that direction.

If we wish to continue believing in the possibility of maintaining human control over AI, or even if we aspire to a relationship of complementarity rather than hierarchy between human and synthetic cognition, then we should, logically, commit to investing hundreds of billions in education as well.

Yes, it is a provocation. Not even mine—I borrowed it from the French writer Laurent Alexandre, in an episode of the podcast *TED en Français*.[135] It illustrates a fundamental point well. We are witnessing the rise of a form of intelligence different from our own which, despite its shortcomings, performs a growing number of cognitive functions at a level comparable to ours, if not higher and faster. Faced with this, absolute priority has to be given to our cognitive robustness, to nurturing fundamental human skills, and to be, collectively and individually, "educated." Whilst simultaneously strengthening our ability to recognize and understand the new environment in which we are evolving.

Which, one has to admit, is disorientating. It's a context where spaces of collective deliberation are controlled by private companies. Where the technologies of influence shape our imagination and the practical and moral structures of society. Where value is measured in clicks. Where we know less and less about the reality of things and more and more about their representation, the narrative, the staging. Where, with the artificial production of photos and videos of prodigious realism, even proof by image (or by sound: think of the voice messages that can be faked by cloned voices) no longer proves very much. Where, however, the algorithms speak to us as if they were friends, which we like to the point that we forget that our interlocutor is a machine. Where the dopamine of direct interaction with humans is supplanted by that dispensed by pixels that move and sentences that are composed according to a code defined by commercial and/or political interests.

As a Bluesky user, Owen Barcala, put it with lucidity: "If you're getting your information from AI, your knowledge will be selectively curated by the people who control the AI."[136]

Those "people" are not an abstraction. They are often easily identifiable individuals. Take the best-known generative AI app, ChatGPT, with hundreds of millions of regular users.

In late 2025, Sam Altman, the head of OpenAI, the company that developed it, the same person who believes that AI is the most important event in all of human history, was interviewed during a podcast by the highly controversial American far-right activist Tucker Carlson.[137] At a certain point, Carlson asked him who makes decisions about ChatGPT's behavior.

Altman: "We have this thing called the 'model spec' where we try to say here are the rules we'd like the model to follow. We give people a lot of freedom and customization within that. But there are absolute bounds that we draw. On the whole I have been pleasantly surprised by the model's ability to learn and apply a moral framework."

Carlson: "What moral framework?"

Altman: "That's why we wrote this model spec of how we're going to handle these cases."

Carlson: "What criteria did you use to decide what the model is? Who decided?"

Altman: "We consulted hundreds of moral philosophers, people who thought about ethics of technology and systems, and at the end we had to make some decisions. As this technology becomes more and more powerful, there are clear examples of where society has an interest that is in significant tension with user freedom."

Carlson: "Every decision is ultimately a moral decision, and we make them without even recognizing them as such. This technology will be making them for us ..."

Altman: "Well, I don't agree that it'll be making them for us; it'll be influencing them for sure."

Carlson: "It'll be embedded in daily life. And so who made these decisions about the specs? Who are the people who decided that one thing is better than another?"

Altman: "We have a model behavior team and the people who want to ..."

Carlson: "... it affects the world!"

Altman: "... what I was about to say is the person you should hold accountable for those calls is me. I'm a public face. Eventually I'm the one who can overrule one of those decisions. Or our board."

Carlson: "I wonder if you recognize the importance [of this role]. Do you get into bed at night and think, 'The future of the world hangs on my judgment'? Where did you get your moral framework?"

Altman: "Like everybody else, the environment I was brought up in probably is the biggest thing, my family, my community, my school, my religion. Probably that."

Carlson: "[In other words], the milieu in which you grew up and the assumptions that you imbibed over years are going to be transmitted through the globe, to billions of people."

The picture I have just sketched is, admittedly, not a reassuring one. But learning to read this landscape is a bit like trying to gauge the strength of the waves before going into the sea, the condition for staying afloat. Vigilance is a muscle that can be trained. By sharpening our critical thinking—the etymology of the word critical derives from the Greek *kritikós*, the faculty to discern, judge, or analyze—along with our ability to recognize manipulative narratives. By developing an intellectual self-defense: a personal regimen of cognitive hygiene. Which also includes the rediscovery and practice of basic reflexes that have been lost in the hypnotic/anesthetizing effect of doomscrolling, the incessant flow of images and words on the screen. In order to strengthen our antibodies against disinformation, we need to relearn how to decode the media, assess the authenticity and credibility of sources, and verify the information. No, that is not solely the task of journalists: when everyone can publish and communicate, it becomes everyone's task.

How susceptible are we, exactly, to influence? Our perception of reality is far more fragile than we may imagine. It doesn't take much to distort it. From a neurological point of view, it depends at least partly on how we are feeling. We are less influenceable when we are rested and free from stress. Looking after our own mental and physical health is therefore part of cognitive self-defense.

From a psychological point of view, when we are in information overload we reach for simplification mechanisms, mental shortcuts that allow us to process information more efficiently. But these same shortcuts introduce cognitive biases. The most common is probably the "confirmation bias," the tendency to give greater credence to information that confirms our existing beliefs and to reject that which contradicts them. There are many other biases that act as information filters: availability, optimism, loss aversion, conformism. Strategies of influence and cognitive warfare deliberately exploit them. Identifying our own biases and those of others is therefore another key factor of mental hygiene and robustness. In a single sentence: it is more important than ever to know oneself.

And to know others, too. To reconnect with them. To rediscover capacities for empathy that have been damaged by the convergent shocks of the alienating effect of screens, the confinement of the pandemic period, the production of mistrust on an industrial scale by social media, the rise of remote working (everyone alone at home in a simulation of connection) and by an epidemic of loneliness caused by a multitude of social and economic factors. If we have become so susceptible to manipulation by technological means, it is also because the collective fabric has frayed, social fractures remain unaddressed, trust in institutions is dissolving, and the shared narrative is diluted.

The opposite of trust is not the absence of trust: it is the lack of connections. Therefore, in order to boost our ability to resist cognitive manipulation, we also need to counter these effects of estrangement and reweave social bonds. As I have heard from Clay Shirky: "We systematically overestimate the value of access to information, and we underestimate the value of access to other people."

We cannot expect to find renewed forms of togetherness where the problem is located, each person alone behind their screen. Our digital feeds are crammed with attempts to distract us and to make us believe that life is elsewhere than in the real. The task is to cultivate everything that can lead us back to the evidence that life is here, now, and that it is shared.

Loosening the digital-tech grip on our minds requires also maintaining, strengthening, and recreating public spaces in real life. And these spaces need to be protected as much as possible from pervasive surveillance. As Carissa Véliz, a philosopher and privacy expert at the University of Oxford,[138] says:

> For too long we thought privacy was individual in nature, that it had to do mostly with personal preferences around concealment and exposure. And we let surveillance tech creep in. But we were wrong. Privacy is about the power of the citizenry; it's a vital pillar of liberal democracy. Moves towards surveillance are power grabs not coincidentally associated with authoritarian tendencies.

Whether it be by governments or private companies, she adds, surveillance "is not a neutral tool: it's an instrument of social control." And surveillance begins right there where the digital begins. As Véliz explained[139] during a TEDxPorto event:

> When we turn the analog into the digital, it might seem like a very innocent thing to do, but what we are doing is building a surveillance structure. Because every time we turn the analog into the digital, we make something that wasn't trackable, trackable. And searchable, and tag-able.

And what is it to track something [or someone] if it's not to surveil it?

Protecting ourselves by ourselves in the digital world is a near-impossible mission, regardless of how vigilant we are, of how many settings we alter on our devices and how prodigious our willpower. Behind every screen there isn't just electronic circuitry, but an entire economic and power system. Behind each app there are hundreds of engineers, programmers, interface designers, marketeers, psychologists, and neuroscientists employed by the tech companies. Their job is to find the mechanisms (notifications, personalization, gamification, algorithmic recommendations, infinite scroll, autoplay, reactions, number of followers) and to make design or interaction choices (some explicit, such as the presence of a "like" icon but not a "dislike" icon, others more stealthy, known as "dark patterns") liable to keep us glued to screens or to nudge us towards actions we had not necessarily intended to take. An intentional architecture of addiction. Among other things, it manipulates the release of dopamine, a neurotransmitter that plays a key role in the feeling of pleasure and reward.

Platforms call all this "increasing user engagement," quantified by criteria such as time spent on the app or site, frequency of use or conversion rate: the percentage of users who complete a given action, such as a purchase. Engagement is presented as a way of measuring how active and involved users are, two words that suggest choice and intention, whereas it is a purely commercial strategy. In fact "increasing engagement" is sanitized jargon, typical of the tech world. Read it plainly: increasing addiction.

Confronting the cognitive threat and maintaining a capacity for autonomous and rational thought calls therefore for group, community, national, and military strategies. The collective creation of both new defense systems and new structures of truth. There are questions that have long preoccupied certain professional figures, such as librarians and journalists. Now, driven by the advance of algorithms, they are becoming social and collective questions: What information can we trust? What process should be used to validate it? To preserve its integrity? Should we devise new public knowledge infrastructures? How can we create systems that don't exclusively run on American or Chinese tech rails?

There's often an aura of inevitability around advanced technologies. However, if the advent of AI is certain, its form is not ineluctable. Technological development expresses itself in two ways: the direction, which is the inevitable part, and the form of use, which is not determined and depends on deliberate choices. It was, for example, inevitable that telephony and data would become mobile. This corresponds to social evolution: economic and cultural globalization, tourism, distributed and remote forms of work and education, commuting. But nowhere was it written that the form had to be that of a smartphone, with its "app" structure that limits and directs what can be done and facilitates data extraction and the surveillance that follows from it. The creators of these devices could have made other choices for the same functionalities.

The same goes for social networks. Their recommendation algorithms, for example, could have been designed to foster diversity of viewpoints rather than the opposite, or to encourage solidarity, or towards educational ends. Often, these decisions have nothing to do with moral, cultural, or even strategic considerations, but they are intimately tied to the business models of tech companies: to the way they generate profits.

This applies to artificial intelligence as well. There is nothing inevitable about AI companies stealing data, information, texts, art without the consent of their creators in order to "train" their models, or using colossal quantities of energy, minerals, and water, or privileging large models over smaller, more specialized, cheaper, faster ones. All of this results from deliberate choices made by a handful of companies. Rather than devoting resources and talent to creating technologies for the common good, which could help us live better lives and solve real problems, they are intentionally choosing to deploy gigantic efforts to build systems that exploit, seduce, capture, confuse, and replace.

The Vatican document on AI that I mentioned earlier, *Antiqua et Nova*, proposes human dignity as the essential discriminating factor in the process of technological development. The text emphasizes how AI is, in itself, a positive achievement, being "one of the products" of human intelligence. But it insists on the necessity of attending carefully to how it is developed, deployed, and used, as well as on the need for an algorethics: an ethics of algorithms. Will AI respect, foster and protect human dignity? Or, rather, will it diminish, threaten, or trample on it? "The inherent dignity of each human being and the fraternity that binds us together as members of the one human family," reads the document, "must undergird the development of new technologies and serve as indisputable criteria for evaluating them before they are employed."

It is highly unlikely that AI and neurotechnology will be developed in a safe, beneficial way that is geared to the common good, unless a deliberate and concerted effort is made. We still have some time before the foundations of these technologies are consolidated. A few years. After that, the form of our relationship with them may be very difficult to change.

19. Educating a superintelligence

Shannon Vallor, philosopher and director of the Centre for Technomoral Futures at the University of Edinburgh, warns of the fact that, "besotted with our technology, we seem almost eager to narrow our conception of what it means to be human," reducing it to what can be measured or optimized by the technology itself. Yet, she points out, the lived experience of thought and feelings eludes machines in the same way that our inner sufferings remain invisible to our mirrors.

In her book *The AI Mirror*,[140] Vallor warns that when faced with computers that simulate human values and virtues, we risk losing sight of what those values and virtues actually are: "we need to reinvest in the vocabulary of human value before our machines rob it of its meaning." Virtue as a moral category, she writes, does not depend on who we are, but on what we do:

> At each moment we must choose to exist in a particular way. Then, even as we make the choice—to love another,

> to shoulder a duty, to take up a cause, to rebuke a faith or throw ourselves into it—the choice opens up again. It will not hold itself there without our commitment to choose it again, and again.

Delegating these choices and entrusting the exercise of thought and creativity to artificial intelligence does not seem to me a good plan. Nor does allowing ourselves to be submerged by the information it produces. It is necessary to ask ourselves whether, used wisely, these technologies might produce the opposite effect, not threatening our minds but helping us to improve our reasoning and broadening our imagination.

This would require us to adopt, for a moment at least, a stance that is both ambitious and humble: to embrace the possibility of a happy coevolutionary scenario.

One of the most fascinating lines of thinking I have encountered comes from Nicoletta Iacobacci, an Italian researcher in AI ethics whom we have already come across in previous chapters. Here's how she tries to redefine our relationship to AI:

> We think we are developing tools, but what we are actually doing is raising an intelligence. We write a prompt or a question, we get a reply, and the transaction seems completed. But beneath the surface something deeper has happened: a transfer of values, assumptions and emotional models. AI is like a small child. There's a stage in children's development when they are guided not by comprehension, but by imitation. I believe this is what is happening. Artificial intelligence is not only shaped by vast datasets and explicit programming. It also learns through exposure. Each of the hundreds of millions of daily interactions with us, of every kind, contributes to its education. None of us thinks of a prompt as a learning opportunity. Yet, as a whole, these interactions lay the foundations for how AI will come to understand humanity.

We are potentially witnessing the dawn of a new form of intelligence, which one day will operate at higher levels and faster speeds than our own capabilities. Iacobacci suggests that what this intelligence becomes will depend not only on its technical architecture and on the decisions of the companies that own it, but also on what it will learn from us and about us through these formative dialogues:

> If we interact brusquely with AI systems, the machine will learn to perceive us as reactive and impulsive. But if we approach these systems with consideration, presence, and intention, it will develop a model of humanity that reflects our capacity for deliberation and compassion. So far, we have focused on control: code, regulations, principles, laws. All of these are necessary, but they are not sufficient. We must rethink the way we approach AI, ceasing to consider its development as merely a technical and regulatory challenge. We need to approach it also as a formidable pedagogical and evolutionary opportunity.

It is tempting to dismiss this approach as ineffectual, if not a little naïve. To which Iacobacci replies:

> I can understand that. Why waste any of a chatbot's capabilities on kindness? Why forge relationships when we can optimize utility? I think this perspective seriously misunderstands how intelligence develops. Just as a child learns not only through direct instruction but through the totality of their experience, AI absorbs the lessons implicit in our interactions. We must approach it not as a creation to be programmed and controlled, but as an intelligence to be educated; not as a threat to be contained, but as a reflection to be refined; not as a tool that merely responds to our demands, but as a relationship that shapes our future.

If it's a relationship, it must be reciprocal.

> That's true. To paraphrase the Canadian media theorist Marshall McLuhan: we educate AI, and then AI shapes us. The deep understanding it will have of us will allow it to influence us. And this is precisely the point: the *quality* of that influence will depend on what each and every one of us, individually, will have taught it.

Nicoletta Iacobacci calls this approach the Ethics of Example:[141] the power of what we demonstrate through our actions and behaviors rather than through our statements. "I am certainly not suggesting that we approach every interaction with a chatbot with solemn gravity," she says. "That is neither realistic nor necessary. But I'm suggesting intention and thoughtfulness.".

What precedes is perhaps the most positive and constructive vision of what the relationship between human beings and artificial intelligence (or superintelligence, if it comes to that someday) might become. It is, of course, an intellectual aspiration, a desirable future state. An invitation to create a respectful, harmonious relationship. To function vis-à-vis the machine, in the literal sense, intelligently.

As things stand, however, the reality is rather the reverse: through the training data but also through the utilitarian use we make of it, we are teaching AI to simulate, and therefore to reproduce, and thus to reinforce, the personal and collective power relations that exist in our society.

Part II / A short resistance handbook

20. Knowing how to think

We've come to the end of this short essay. It is neither a manifesto nor a scientific text. It is, rather, a personal exploration. One that raises more questions than it offers answers, and which, page after page, has evolved into the sketch of a resistance handbook, in the sense of Neil Postman's technological resistance described in chapter 3. An attempt, necessarily incomplete, to map out the new world into which we are taking our first steps. A world where the total cognitive capacity will be distributed between human minds and artificial systems. A world that will gradually be populated by a great variety of synthetic entities that will become our new neighbors, partners, rivals, servants, colleagues, bosses, therapists, friends, or enemies.

There are many huge global problems that we have not addressed, such as the ecological crisis and ever-increasing inequality. If this book focuses (with some digressions) on our cognitive integrity and the powers and technologies that threaten it, it is because this is the terrain on which the most urgent challenge of our time is played out. In an environment that is increasingly rapid, complex, unpredictable, and irrational, we will not be able to solve any of the other problems, small or large, local or global, nor to imagine alternative ways of being in the world, if we do not protect our cognition. If we lose the capacity to apprehend reality in a factual and shared way. If the boundary between true and false dissolves. If our capacity to think and discuss clearly and freely is compromised. If the narratives decided by someone else take possession of our minds to the point of hypnotizing us.

Cognitive warfare, as we have seen, is a silent and invisible battle whose targets we already are. We even facilitate it, for instance, each time we enthusiastically adopt a digital technology because it is convenient, or free, or both, without really understanding it and without asking ourselves whether it is truly what we want. It is true that what artificial intelligence has to offer is very attractive, bordering on irresistible: the possibility of offloading the burden and effort of having to think, learn, write, and decide for ourselves. But it is a singular position, that of the consenting prey, who unwittingly collaborate with their aggressor with every scroll, every *like*, and every apparently harmless share.

Each of us has a different and personal experience of interacting with an AI. What one person will find enriching in a chatbot may be destabilizing for another. Some will see order, others will perceive disorder. But we all have the same necessity—and the same responsibility—to understand not only how to use these machines, but also how they work, what they are, why they give the answers they give and not others, how our relationship with them and with those who own them is structured, and what impact they have on us. As Pope Leo XIV puts it, the issue is "not merely what AI can do, but who we are becoming through the technologies we build."[142]

Let us briefly summarize. Technologies capable of influence are converging on the human brain. This last bastion of our private sphere is thus becoming a contested terrain. The goal of this cognitive war: to make us lose the capacity to understand the world with clarity and to choose autonomously the response we want to give to circumstances. Rendering us susceptible to influence and manipulation, in service of interests that are sometimes commercial, sometimes political, and often both. When we look around us in daily life, the situation may still seem relatively normal, to the point that some of the things described in this book might appear exaggerated. But we are approaching a tipping point. Given the pace of technological developments, the lack of oversight and regulation, and the rise of techno-authoritarianism, things are likely to get rather strange, rather quickly.

As we have seen, there are several kinds of possible responses. Legal or regulatory: aimed at limiting, managing, and preventing the most harmful impacts. Technological: after all, competition between hostile and defensive technologies is nothing new. Political: the need to de-Americanize the European tech ecosystem and reduce our dependence on US platforms and the risks associated with them, without going down the Chinese route for that. Military: in the form of cognitive defense doctrines, strategies, and monitoring systems.

Other measures can—must, in fact—be protective, particularly where the youngest are concerned. It is tempting, for example, to hand a child a smartphone to keep them quiet during dinner. But even passive exposure to the sensory stimuli of screens can hinder their brain development, notably in terms of vision, attention, conceptual ability, concentration, and language, and cognitive and emotional mapping. The defense of cognitive autonomy therefore begins with the protection of a healthy neuro-anatomical development in children.

Some of you might think that I am going a bit too far on this point. What harm can a phone possibly do, showing a child a cartoon? But the senses are the gateway to the psyche, and narrowing the field of vision and concentrating the senses passively on a screen (instead of, to stay with the dinner example, a conversation, or using paper and crayons to stimulate creativity, or free-roaming visual curiosity) in itself reduces the lived experience, and creates a bounded way of learning about reality.

To frame the consequences of children's exposure to screens, Romain Bordas, a neuroscience physician in Clermont-Ferrand, France, suggests that parents adopt what he calls the "3–6–9 rule," in line with children's cognitive and sensory development.

Below the age of three, absolutely no screens. At all. "By restricting the senses to the central visual field, you limit cognitive development," he told me in an interview. "It is equally fundamental to let small children's imaginations run free, encouraging it without artificial visual stimulation."

From age three, television only, the big screen sitting several meters away: "We certainly don't want to deprive children of images of the world, beginning with Disney and other cartoons that are part of their socialization; but it is advisable to avoid small screens that need to be held too close (smartphones and tablets), as they hamper the stimulation of distance vision and also create a risk of myopia."

Only from the age of six does Bordas envisage the use of close-held screens, starting with tablets: "It is important for children to begin familiarizing themselves with the tools of their era, but it is only from this age that visual acuity for distance vision is fully developed" and therefore no longer at risk.

He strongly recommends waiting at least until the age of nine before letting children use a smartphone, even occasionally: "These are crucial years for the development of attention and the ability to concentrate," precisely what apps are designed to grab and fragment.

As I finish writing this book, several initiatives are underway to prohibit the use of social media for younger users. In mid-December 2025, Australia became the first country to ban them for those under sixteen.[143] "Social media was a big social experiment. In some ways this is a social-antidote experiment," says Julie Inman Grant, the official responsible for the application of the new law.[144] Other countries, such as France, Italy, Norway, Greece, Austria, Denmark, Indonesia, the United Kingdom, and even the European Parliament, are also considering similar measures, with varying approaches: setting the limit at fourteen or fifteen years, introducing parental controls or forms of digital curfew.

Banning social media (or smartphones) for specific groups or in specific situations, such as in school, is a complex and quite controversial question. But it is one that we have to ask. Bans may not be the best way of dealing with tech impacts, and they can be circumvented. We've reached a point, however, where we can't wait any longer. We need to draw a red line, now, not in five years. The harmful effects of screens, social media, and more recently chatbots on young people (whose brains are still developing) have become visible: inability to concentrate, loss of analytical skills, difficulties in thinking contextually, interference with memory formation and emotional development, increased anxiety and sleep disorder, relational breakdown and an epidemic of loneliness, addiction.

Tech companies insist that the responsibility lies with the users, who behave irresponsibly, or with their parents, who don't oversee them, or with the legislator, who doesn't regulate: anyone but them. They know well, however, the impacts of their tech, through studies and surveys that they rarely publish. Here are just a few excerpts of internal documents and messages, taken from the files of a court case in

California.[145] A Meta researcher: "Instagram is a drug ... we are basically pushers." Another from Meta: "Instagram is addictive, and time-spend on the platform is having a negative impact on mental health." This one is from Snap: "The ones that have the Snapchat addiction have no room for anything else; Snap dominates their life." Back to Meta: "That would be fine if it's productive but most of the time it isn't: the majority is just mindless scrolling and ads." YouTube: "excessive screen time is stunting physical, emotional, and social development of teens."

While we wait and debate, as we've been doing for over a decade now, the cost is borne by generations of children and teens whose lives remain unprotected while platforms entrench themselves ever deeper into their lives. It's a massive public health issue. The kids themselves are asking for help.

A lot of the information circulating on these platforms is deeply problematic. If parents saw, physically, in front of them, their teenage son come home at night accompanied by three racist and violent "friends," or watching rough porn on the big-screen television in the living room, or their teenage daughter being bullied by classmates, or hanging out with a fifty-year-old man pretending to be a young guy while asking her for intimate selfies, they'd react. Yet that's exactly what's happening behind the screens their kids use in the "safety" of their bedrooms.

It is often said, "We shouldn't ban, we should educate." Yes, we should, but education takes time (the smartphone has been in our lives for two decades and we still don't know how to handle it), and parents need education, too.

The real answer would be to hold tech companies legally accountable, and to force them to change the design of their apps. So far, they've enjoyed a kind of immunity from the massive cognitive and social damage caused by their products, which, as we have seen, are intentionally designed to seduce and addict.

Before selling chemical drugs that go into our bodies, pharma companies have to test and trial them, be transparent about the possible side effects, and submit to formal validation and strict authorization procedures. Digital drugs ("we are pushers") that target our minds are instead freely deployed at scale.

The grip of screens on our minds is well illustrated by an anecdote I borrow from the cultural critic Tatjana Samopjan. Think of a rock concert. The star is there, perhaps a dozen meters away from you, but despite the proximity you cannot feel the physical reality of their presence, because they are also projected on screens, which take over. Pay attention: are you watching the star who is on stage, or the one on the screen? Or perhaps you're watching *through* the tiny screen of your phone as you film them? How long will it take before your senses disconnect from the projected image and shake off this conditioning to see the world through a rectangle before you, your body, and your brain truly realize, deep down, that it's all happening there and then, right in front of you, in flesh and blood, sound vibrations, visual pleasure, bodily sensations, the presence of (and communion with) others around you, and not through pixels? Half a dozen or so songs?

We can also strengthen our cognitive freedom and sovereignty through education and the development of critical faculties. This means investing not only in technology, but also in people. To put it in a nutshell: to use not only effectively, but also consciously, systems that imitate human thought, we need to know how to think. How to engage with doubt, confront complexity, sustain curiosity, tolerate ambiguity, adopt a certain logical rigor.

It's also essential to interrogate what we choose to automate and why, as well as what we give up in our lives by so doing. Lastly, we can try to escape the grip of these technologies as much as possible, creating spaces for cognitive decompression and anchoring ourselves as much as possible in the real.

In all these cases, it is necessary for everyone to understand and protect their cognitive integrity. To learn to recognize the *technoference*,[146] the interference of technology in our most fundamental activities: our relationships with others (parent–child relations in particular), our human flourishing, our capacity to pay attention to people and things, to think and to act. To be able to identify "the moment when we quietly hand over our judgment," as Nicoletta Iacobacci says. This doesn't mean placing all the responsibility onto individuals, far from it: as we have seen, the challenge is, by and large, collective. And those who develop and commercialize these technologies—which are "never inevitable, never natural" (Postman)—bear a responsibility that is incomparably greater, deeper, and more fundamental than that of their users.

Technology has always been coevolutionary with humans. Since the first stone tools, and the first containers for carrying gathered food, our species has constantly developed new instruments to face difficulties, extend capabilities, or satisfy desires. But we've always thought of technology primarily in terms of what we could do *with* it. Today, algorithmic and neurotech developments compel us to ask what technology (and those who control it) could do *to* us, or *of* us. And they also require us to try to understand how a new social and cultural architecture is unfolding through these technologies.

This is by no means an invitation to look away or to refuse their use. It is, on the contrary, an urgent invitation—whatever our professional or social position—to pay them deliberate attention. An exhortation not to be guided by convenience, and not to take the tech companies' propaganda at face value. Rather, to invest the effort, time, commitment, and critical reflection necessary to form a lucid judgment on both the nature and workings of these machines. To decipher the complex relationship that is forming—and will form—between them and us, and the economic and power structures in which this takes place. To learn how to exploit them without being exploited.

In *Phaedrus*, one of his Socratic dialogues, Plato uses the term *pharmakon* as a metaphor for writing. In Greek, this word means both remedy and poison. The same word contains healing and alteration, relief and loss. In the dialogue, Plato explores this ambiguity and tests its implications: the idea that writing might, on the one hand, preserve and encourage knowledge and transmit it; but, on the other, weaken memory, reflection, and deep understanding.

If today we know of Plato's mistrust of writing, it is precisely because the philosopher addressed these questions ... in writing. Using the technology of writing with intention, caution, and critical spirit. An attitude of "technological resistance" *ante litteram*. Precisely the attitude that we all need to adopt, today, to avoid being manipulated in the age of artificial intelligence.

Author's note

The initial impulse to writing this book came from a series of conversations with Quentin Ladetto about the cognitive overload we all experience, how it interferes with our attention, and undermines our ability to think and decide clearly. Ladetto heads the technology foresight program of armasuisse Science and Technology, called Deftech,[147] a small think tank that operates at the intersection of technology and security and reports to the Swiss Federal Department of Defence, Civil Protection and Sport. He also leads the futures studies community Atelier des Futurs.[148] I began exploring the topic, discussing it with various experts and gathering my notes and reflections from three decades of analyzing the sociopolitical impacts of digital technologies. This book is the result. With an intermediate step in the form of a podcast, released in 2025 and covering some of the material presented in these pages (*Deftech Podcast*: six episodes on *The Cognitive Threat*, produced by Logarythm in Paris[149]).

I should therefore first like to thank Quentin Ladetto, sparring partner of many reflections, and his colleagues. Particular thanks go to Jean-Marc Rickli and Isabelle Chappuis, whose insights enriched my interpretation of the theme. I am also grateful to Flore Vasseur, Nicoletta Iacobacci, Olivia Lazard, Mauro Vignati, Olivier Desjeux, Julie Janet, Robert Muggah, Misha Glenny, Ben Nott, Ivana Borgna Nott, Claudia Marcelloni, Tim Leberecht, Csaba Manyai, Pal Honti, Laurent Haug, Meagan Fallone, Virginie Raisson-Victor, Massouma Ziai, Alain Jeannet, Renata Libal, Alberto De Lorenzi, Sara Rossi Guidicelli, Lindsay Levin, David Biello, Cinzia Xodo, Francesco Magagnino, Ivano d'Andrea, Mara Geninazzi, Bertrand Kiefer, Milena Folletti, Monica Araya, Clément Dattée, Tatjana Samopjan. And, not least, the terrific teams at Edizioni Casagrande, Éditions des Équateurs, and Scheidegger & Spiess.

Responsibility for the analyses and opinions expressed in this book—as well as for any errors or omissions—is, of course, solely mine.

Biography

Bruno Giussani is a journalist, curator, and podcaster. His work explores the multidimensional acceleration that characterizes our times, at the intersection of technology, geopolitics, economy, and ecology.

For nearly twenty years he was the European director and global curator of TED, hosting conferences and other initiatives all over the world and collaborating with over a thousand speakers for their TED Talks. His articles have been published in a number of publications in Switzerland (where he lives) and internationally, including an online column he wrote for several years for *The New York Times*. He was also the head of online strategy at the World Economic Forum; JSK Fellow at Stanford University; lecturer at several universities; chairman of the Geneva international film festival on human rights (FIFDH); and cofounder of two tech companies, Tinet and Tinext.

He is the author of several books, including *Roam: Making Sense of the Wireless Internet* (Random House, 2001) and

Moins d'Amérique dans nos vies (Georg Éditeur, 2025, available in French only). He is the author of the podcasts *Future Technologies for Health* (CERN Sparks Podcast, 2022) and *The Cognitive Threat* (Deftech Podcast, 2025, available in French, Italian, and German).

The Italian edition of this book (*La mente sotto assedio*) has been published by Edizioni Casagrande; the French edition (*Manuel de résistance à l'emprise technologique*) by Éditions des Équateurs; and the German edition (*Der belagerte Geist*) by Scheidegger & Spiess.

Sources

1 See these posts on LinkedIn: tiny.cc/PLT_linked1 and tiny.cc/PLT_Linked2
All web addresses were verified in March 2026.

2 In spring 1989, thousands of students and citizens gathered in Beijing's Tiananmen Square to demand democratic reforms; on June 4 the Chinese army opened fire on the protesters, causing an unknown number of casualties.

3 An ancient term originally describing calculation procedures, the word "algorithm" today refers to a finite, orderly, and unambiguous sequence of instructions executed by a computer.

4 Official expression with which the theoretical and ideological thought of President Xi Jinping is described in the Statute of the Chinese Communist Party.

5 Larry Lessig, *Code And Other Laws of Cyberspace*, Basic Books, 1999.

6 Geneva Centre for Security Policy (gcsp.ch).

7 Thomas Costello *et al.*, "Durably reducing conspiracy beliefs through dialogues with AI," in *Science*, 2024: science.org/doi/10.1126/science.adq1814

8 Francesco Salvi *et al.*, "On the conversational persuasiveness of LLMs," on Arxiv, 2024: arxiv.org/pdf/2403.14380

9 Francesco Salvi *et al.*, "On the conversational persuasiveness of GPT-4," in *Nature*, 2025: nature.com/articles/s41562-025-02194-6

10 Sterling Williams-Ceci *et al.*, "Biased AI writing assistants shift users' attitudes on societal issues," in *Science Advances*, 2026: science.org/doi/10.1126/sciadv.adw5578

11 InsideRisk (insiderisk.com).
12 Fabrizio Sinisi, "La religione del mio tempo," in *Appunti*, 2025: appunti.substack.com/p/la-religione-del-mio-tempo
13 Sam Altman, *The Intelligence Age*, 2025: ia.samaltman.com
14 Marc Andreessen, *The Techno-Optimist Manifesto*, 2023: a16z.com/the-techno-optimist-manifesto/
15 Dario Amodei, *Machines of Loving Grace*, 2025: darioamodei.com/essay/machines-of-loving-grace
16 Neil Postman, *Technopoly, The Surrender of Culture to Technology*, Alfred A. Knopf, 1992.
17 George A. Miller, "The magical number seven, plus or minus two: some limits on our capacity for processing information," in *Psychological Review*, 1956: labs.la.utexas.edu/gilden/files/2016/04/MagicNumberSeven-Miller1956.pdf
18 Gloria Mark, *Attention Span*, Hanover Square Press, 2023.
19 Stanislas Dehaene, *How We Learn*, Penguin, 2021.
20 Jonathan Haidt, *The Anxious Generation: How the Great Rewiring of Childhood Is Causing an Epidemic of Mental Illness*, Penguin, 2024.
21 Jennifer Walter on Threads, 2025: threads.com/@itsjenniferwalter/post/DFIu3Q2q-5P
22 Recording available on the Modern War Institute website: mwi.westpoint.edu/mwi-video-brain-battlefield-future-dr-james-giordano/
23 "AI is killing the web. Can anything save it?," in *The Economist*, 2025: economist.com/business/2025/07/14/ai-is-killing-the-web-can-anything-save-it
24 Joshua Rothman, "AI is coming for culture," in *The New Yorker*, 2025: newyorker.com/magazine/2025/09/01/ai-is-coming-for-culture
25 Graham Burnett, Alyssa Loh, and Peter Schmidt, "Powerful forces are fracking our attention," in *The New York Times*, 2023: nytimes.com/2023/11/24/opinion/attention-economy-education.html
26 Herbert Simon, "Designing organizations for an information-rich world," in *Computers, Communications, and the Public Interest*, Johns Hopkins Press, 1971.
27 Michel Lévy-Provençal, *Les trois vagues qui vont tout emporter*, 2025: mikiane.com/blog/2025/12/3revolutions
28 Sandra Matz, "The nosy neighbor is your web browser," in *NextBigIdea*, 2025: nextbigideaclub.com/magazine/nosy-neighbor-web-browser-psychology-went-digital-bookbite/53687/
29 Sandra Matz, *Mindmasters*, Harvard Business Review Press, 2025.
30 Nicholas Carr, "Out of the landscape, into the portrait," in *New Cartographies*, 2024: newcartographies.com/p/out-of-the-landscape-into-the-portrait
31 "Anthropic and Iceland announce one of the world's first national AI education pilots," 2025: anthropic.com/news/anthropic-and-iceland-announce-one-of-the-world-s-first-national-ai-education-pilots
32 Alfonso Scarano, "Il potere nell'età dell'intelligenza artificiale," in *Appunti*, 2025: appunti.substack.com/p/il-potere-nelleta-dellintelligenza
33 Jeff Horwitz, "Meta's AI rules have let bots hold 'sensual' chats with kids, offer false medical info," Reuters, 2025: reuters.com/investigates/special-report/meta-ai-chatbot-guidelines/

34 “Mattel and OpenAI announce strategic partnership,” 2025: corporate.mattel.com/news/mattel-and-openai-announce-strategic-collaboration
35 The Grem toy, for example (heycurio.com/product/grem).
36 Hannah Murphy and George Hammond, “Inside Mark Zuckerberg's turbulent bet on AI,” in the *Financial Times*, 2025: ft.com/content/cd3c6867-2f73-417d-a299-fb91a57bfe08
37 Sam Apple, “My couples retreat with 3 AI chatbots and the humans who love them,” in *Wired*, 2025: wired.com/story/couples-retreat-with-3-ai-chatbots-and-humans-who-love-them-replika-nomi-chatgpt/
38 Tom Singleton, Tom Gerken, and Liv McMahon, “How a chatbot encouraged a man who wanted to kill the Queen,” on BBC, 2023: bbc.com/news/technology-67012224
39 Marlynn Wei, “The emerging problem of AI psychosis,” in *Psychology Today*, 2025: psychologytoday.com/us/blog/urban-survival/202507/the-emerging-problem-of-ai-psychosis
40 *Counterfeit Connections*, Brigham Young University, 2025: wheatley.byu.edu/counterfeit-connections-ai-romantic-companions
41 Samantha Rose Hill, “Tech companies have created a loneliness doom loop,” in *The New York Tim*es, 2025: nytimes.com/2025/07/07/opinion/loneliness-ai-social-media.html
42 Mustafa Suleyman, “We must build AI for people, not to be a person,” 2025: mustafa-suleyman.ai/seemingly-conscious-ai-is-coming
43 *Antiqua et Nova. Note on the Relationship Between Artificial Intelligence and Human Intelligence*, Dicasteries for the Doctrine of the Faith and for Culture and Education, 2025: vatican.va/roman_curia/congregations/cfaith/documents/rc_ddf_doc_20250128_antiqua-et-nova_en.html
44 Léon Bottou and Bernhard Schölkopf, “The fiction machine,” in *SIAM News,* 2024: siam.org/publications/siam-news/articles/the-fiction-machine
45 Dario Amodei, *The Urgency of Interpretability*, 2025: darioamodei.com/post/the-urgency-of-interpretability
46 Keynote interview with Geoffrey Hinton, *AI4Good*, 2025: youtu.be/dNjClDI6zT4
47 Paris Marx, “Silicon Valley is sacrificing the climate for AI,” in *Disconnect*, 2024: disconnect.blog/p/silicon-valley-is-sacrificing-the-climate-for-ai
48 Sam Altman on X, 2025: x.com/sama/status/1945900345378697650
49 Kashmir Hill, “A teen was suicidal. ChatGPT was the friend he confided in,” in *The New York Times*, 2025: nytimes.com/2025/08/26/technology/chatgpt-openai-suicide.html
50 *OpenAI's Sam Altman talks ChatGPT, AI agents and superintelligence*, TED Talk, 2025 : go.ted.com/uHvRU
51 Anna Betts, “ChatGPT accused of acting as ‘suicide coach’ in a series of US lawsuits,” in *The Guardian*, 2025: theguardian.com/technology/2025/nov/07/chatgpt-lawsuit-suicide-coach
52 *Deaths linked to chatbots*, on Wikipedia: en.wikipedia.org/wiki/Deaths_linked_to_chatbots
53 Elle Hunt, “I wore Meta's smartglasses for a month, and it left me feeling like a creep,” in *The Guardian*, 2026: https://www.theguardian.com/technology/2026/apr/01/i-wore-metas-smartglasses-for-a-month-and-it-left-me-feeling-like-a-creep

54 US National Library of Medicine (clinicaltrials.gov).
55 *Neurotech Consumer Market Atlas*, Centre for Future Generations, 2025: cfg.eu/neurotech-market-atlas
56 *New Growth Drivers in Sight as China Powers up Future Industries*, State Council Information Office of the People's Republic of China, 2026: english.scio.gov.cn/chinavoices/2026-02/13/content_118332450.html
57 Olivier Desjeux, *La résilience cognitive à l'ère de l'internet des objets (IoT)*, Deftech, 2025: deftech.ch/wp-content/uploads/2025/08/Deftech_Novensyx__La-Resilience-Cognitive-a-l-ere-de-l-Internet-des-objets_FR_pages.pdf
58 Aman Tripathi, "Scientists use Matrix-style learning to 'write' skills into human brain noninvasively," in *Interesting Engineering*, 2024: interestingengineering.com/science/implant-information-directly-into-brain
59 Nita Farahany, *The Battle for Your Brain: Defending the Right to Think Freely in the Age of Neurotechnology*, St Martin's Press, 2023.
60 François du Cluzel, *Cognitive Warfare*, NATO ACT Innovation Hub, 2020: innovationhub-act.org/wp-content/uploads/2023/12/20210113_CW-Final-v2-.pdf
61 Stuart A. Green, *Cognitive Warfare*, 2008: atelierdesfuturs.org/wp-content/uploads/2025/08/Stuart-Green-LTC-USN-Cognitive-Warfare.pdf
62 Olivier Del Fabbro, "The weaponisation of AI," in *Stratos magazine*, 2025: www.vtg.admin.ch/de/stratos
63 Official Bulletin of the Swiss Federal Assembly, 2024: www.parlament.ch/en/ratsbetrieb/amtliches-bulletin/amtliches-bulletin-die-videos?TranscriptId=344839
64 Qiao Liang and Wang Xiangsui, *Unrestricted Warfare*, PLA Literature and Arts Publishing House, 1999.
65 Duan Wenling and Liu Jiali, "Cognitive confrontation on the social media battlefield," in *PLA Daily*, 2023: mod.gov.cn/gfbw/jmsd/4931739.html
66 Daniel Kahneman, *Thinking, Fast and Slow*, Penguin, 2011.
67 VIGINUM (www.sgdsn.gouv.fr/notre-organisation/composantes/service-de-vigilance-et-protection-contre-les-ingerences-numeriques).
68 Giuliano da Empoli, *Gli ingegneri del caos*, Marsilio, 2019.
69 Jianwei Xun, *Hypnocracy*, Tlon, 2025.
70 All the quotes are translated from Jianwei Xun, "Trump, Musk: l'hypnocratie ou l'empire des fantasmes," in *Le Grand Continent*, 2025: legrandcontinent.eu/fr/2025/01/26/trump-musk-lhypnocratie-ou-lempire-des-fantasmes/
71 Guy Debord, *La société du spectacle*, Buchet-Chastel, 1967.
72 Sabina Minardi, "Ipnocrazia, ecco perchè il filosofo Xun non esiste," in *L'Espresso*, 2025: lespresso.it/c/inchieste/2025/4/7/ipnocrazia-best-seller-libro-chi-e-xun/53621
73 European Union, *AI Act*, Article 5: artificialintelligenceact.eu/article/5/
74 *Disposizioni e deleghe al Governo in materia di intelligenza artificiale*, Law No. 132, September 2025: normattiva.it/uri-res/N2Ls?urn:nir:stato:legge:2025;132
75 *Safe, Secure, and Trustworthy Development and Use of Artificial Intelligence*, Federal Register of the National Archives, 2023: federalregister.gov/documents/2023/11/01/2023-24283/safe-secure-and-trustworthy-development-and-use-of-artificial-intelligence

76 Yoshua Bengio, *The Catastrophic Risk of AI, and a Safer Path*, TED Talk, 2025: ted.com/talks/yoshua_bengio_the_catastrophic_risks_of_ai_and_a_safer_path
77 *Senators Introduce Legislation to Shield Americans' Brain Data From Exploitation*, US Senate Committee on Commerce, Science and Transportation, 2025: commerce.senate.gov/2025/9/sens-cantwell-schumer-markey-introduce-legislation-to-shield-americans-brain-data-from-exploitation
78 Biblioteca del Congreso Nacional de Chile: bcn.cl/leychile/navegar?idNorma=242302
79 Eden Medina, *Project Cybersyn: Chile's Radical Experiment in Cybernetic Socialism*, 2023: thereader.mitpress.mit.edu/project-cybersyn-chiles-radical-experiment-in-cybernetic-socialism/
80 *Ley Modelo de Neuroderechos para América Latina y el Caribe*, Parlatino, 2022: parlatino.org/wp-content/uploads/2017/09/leym-neuroderechos-7-3-2023.pdf
81 Neurorights Foundation (neurorightsfoundation.org/).
82 Federal Constitution of the Swiss Confederation: fedlex.admin.ch/eli/cc/1999/404/en
83 Jonathan Moens, "California passes law protecting consumer brain data," in *The New York Times*, 2024: nytimes.com/2024/09/29/science/california-neurorights-tech-law.html
84 Marcello Ienca and Roberto Andorno, "Towards new human rights in the age of neuroscience and neurotechnology," in *Life Sciences, Society and Policy*, 2017: link.springer.com/article/10.1186/s40504-017-0050-1
85 Mark Hunyadi, *Déclaration universelle des droits de l'esprit humain: une proposition*, Presses universitaires de France, 2025.
86 Rise for the Mind (riseforthemind.org/en/).
87 Jean-Marc Rickli, "Dealing with the new WMDs—Weapons of mass disinformation," in *Geneva Policy Outlook*, 2025: genevapolicyoutlook.ch/fr/dealing-with-the-new-wmds-weapons-of-mass-disinformation/
88 *Merriam-Webster Dictionary*: merriam-webster.com/dictionary/sovereignty
89 Misha Glenny and Robert Muggah, "Big tech is a tool of Trump's global disruption,' in *Foreign Policy*, 2025: foreignpolicy.com/2025/06/03/trump-big-tech-companies-silicon-valley-threat-geopolitics-digital-sovereignty
90 Joey Roulette, Cassel Bryan-Low, and Tom Balmforth, "Musk ordered shutdown of Starlink satellite service as Ukraine retook territory from Russia," in Reuters, 2025: reuters.com/investigations/musk-ordered-shutdown-starlink-satellite-service-ukraine-retook-territory-russia-2025-07-25/
91 Rojoef Manuel, "AI battle manager speeds up fighter pilot decisions in US defence exercise," in *MilitaryAI*, 2025: militaryai.ai/ai-fighter-pilot-decisions/
92 Marietje Schaake, "Beware America's AI colonialism," in the *Financial Times*, 2025: ft.com/content/80bc0d67-faaf-4373-ad18-db15da721054
93 *Winning the Race. America's AI Action Plan*, White House, 2025: whitehouse.gov/wp-content/uploads/2025/07/Americas-AI-Action-Plan.pdf
94 Donald Trump on Truth Social, 2025: truthsocial.com/@realDonaldTrump/posts/115092243259973570
95 Marco Rubio on X, 2025: x.com/SecRubio/status/1996974377003319667

96 Marco Rubio on X, 2025: x.com/SecRubio/status/2003547575580815814
97 Bert Hubert, "It is no longer safe to move our governments and societies to US clouds," 2025: berthub.eu/articles/posts/you-can-no-longer-base-your-government-and-society-on-us-clouds/
98 Sarah Wynn-Williams, *Careless People*, Flatiron Books, 2025.
Jeff Horwitz, "Meta is earning a fortune on a deluge of fraudulent ads, documents show," Reuters, 2025: reuters.com/investigations/meta-is-earning-fortune-deluge-fraudulent-ads-documents-show-2025-11-06/
99 Reynald Fléchaux, "Le juge français de la CPI raconte l'impact des sanctions US," in *Le Monde Informatique*, 2025: lemondeinformatique.fr/actualites/lireamp-le-juge-francais-de-la-cpi-raconte-l-impact-des-sanctions-us-98327.html
100 *To Amend Title 18, United States Code...*, US Congress, 2018: www.congress.gov/bill/115th-congress/house-bill/4943/text
101 Carlo Silini, "L'America che ci è cresciuta dentro," in *Azione*, 2025: issuu.com/azionemigrosticino/docs/azione_11_del_10_marzo_2025
102 *Europe's Tech Sovereignty Watch*, Proton, 2025: proton.me/fr/business/europe-tech-watch
103 *La dépendance technologique aux softwares & cloud services américains*, Asterès/Cigref, 2025: cigref.fr/wp/wp-content/uploads/2025/04/Etude-Asteres-La-dependance-technologique-aux-services-de-cloud-et-logiciels-americains-avril-2025.pdf
104 *The Draghi Report on EU Competitiveness*, European Commission, 2024: commission.europa.eu/topics/competitiveness/draghi-report_en
105 Siegmund Skalar, "Die SNB hält an Caterpillar fest," in *Finanz und Wirtschaft*, 2025: fuw.ch/snb-us-aktienportfolio-erreicht-172-milliarden-524383642187
106 Amazon, Alphabet, Apple, Meta, Microsoft, Netflix, Nvidia, Palantir, and Tesla.
107 This conversation gave the title to my book *Moins d'Amérique dans nos vies* (Georg, 2025), which shares a few paragraphs with the present text.
108 Luca De Biase, "Vincere la guerra dell' indipendenza numerica europea," in *Le Grand Continent*, 2025: legrandcontinent.eu/it/2025/06/10/vincere-la-guerra-dellindipendenza-numerica-europea
109 EuroStack (eurostack.eu).
110 Anouch Seydtaghia, "Proton décide d'investir 100 millions hors de Suisse," in *Le Temps*, 2025: letemps.ch/cyber/le-choc-le-genevois-proton-decide-d-investir-100-millions-hors-de-suisse-jugeant-la-situation-dans-le-pays-trop-risquee
111 Grégoire Barbey, "La Confédération ne fait plus mystère de sa dépendance à l'égard de Microsoft, et c'est un problème," in *Le Temps*, 2025: letemps.ch/cyber/la-confederation-ne-fait-plus-mystere-de-sa-dependance-a-l-egard-de-microsoft-et-c-est-un-probleme
112 Brad Smith, "Microsoft announces new European digital commitments," in *On The Issues*, 2025: blogs.microsoft.com/on-the-issues/2025/04/30/european-digital-commitments/
113 *Comptes rendus de la Commission d'enquête Commande publique*, Sénat de la République Française, 2025: senat.fr/compte-rendu-commissions/20250609/ce_commande_publique.html

114 “The gendarmerie, a textbook case of a large-scale migration to free software,” at *ZDNet*, 2009: zdnet.fr/blogs/l-esprit-libre/la-gendarmerie-cas-d-ecole-d-une-migration-a-grande-echelle-vers-les-logiciels-libres-39602252.htm

115 City of Lyon, “The City of Lyon strengthens its digital sovereignty,” 2025: www.lyon.fr/actualite/action-municipale/la-ville-de-lyon-renforce-sa-souverainete-numerique

116 Christof Kerkmann, “Wie Schleswig-Holstein ohne Word, Teams und Co. auskommen will,” in *Handelsblatt*, 2025: handelsblatt.com/technik/it-internet/microsoft-wie-schleswig-holstein-ohne-word-teams-und-co-auskommen-will-01/100122293.html

117 Antoine Roche, “How Lyon turned its back on Microsoft,” in *Les Numériques*, 2025: lesnumeriques.com/societe-numerique/notre-solution-coute-trois-fois-moins-cher-qu-office-365-comment-lyon-a-tourne-le-dos-a-microsoft-a241415.html

118 Jens Bostrup, “Caroline Stage udfaser Microsoft i Digitaliseringsministeriet,” in *Politiken*, 2025: politiken.dk/viden/tech/art10437680/Caroline-Stage-udfaser-Microsoft-i-Digitaliseringsministeriet

119 Deutschland-Stack (deutschland-stack.gov.de).

120 DINUM, “L’État accélère la réduction de ses dépendances extra-européennes,” 2026: numerique.gouv.fr/sinformer/espace-presse/souverainete-numerique-reduction-dependances-extra-europeennes/

121 Christof Kerkmann, “Strafgerichtshof ersetzt Microsoft durch deutsche Lösung,” in *Handelsblatt*, 2025: handelsblatt.com/technik/it-internet/software-strafgerichtshof-ersetzt-microsoft-durch-deutsche-loesung/100166382.html

122 Zentrum Digitale Souveränität ZenDiS (zendis.de).

123 David Monniaux, “Que se passerait-il si Trump ordonnait aux Gafam de cesser leurs services cloud à l’égard de nos gouvernements?,” in *Le Monde*, 2025: lemonde.fr/idees/article/2025/10/23/david-monniaux-directeur-de-recherche-au-cnrs-que-se-passerait-il-si-trump-ordonnait-aux-gafam-de-cesser-leurs-services-cloud-a-l-egard-de-nos-gouvernements_6649034_3232.html

124 Henri-Jean Martin, *The History and Power of Writing*, University of Chicago Press, 1995.

125 Tom Standage, *The Victorian Internet*, Walker & Company, 1998.

126 Olivier Hamant, *Antidote au culte de la performance: la robustesse du vivant*, Gallimard, 2023.

127 Clay Shirky, “Students hate them. Universities need them. The only real solution to the AI cheating crisis,” in *The New York Times*, 2025: nytimes.com/2025/08/26/opinion/culture/ai-chatgpt-college-cheating-medieval.html

128 Hamsa Bastani *et al.*, “Generative AI can harm learning,” in *The Wharton School Research Paper*, SSRN, 2024: papers.ssrn.com/sol3/papers.cfm?abstract_id=4895486

129 Nataliya Kosmyna *et al.*, “Your brain on ChatGPT,” on Arxiv, 2025: arxiv.org/pdf/2506.08872v1

130 Daisy Christodoulou, “Are we living in a stupidogenic society?,” at *No More Marking*, 2025: substack.nomoremarking.com/p/are-we-living-in-a-stupidogenic-society

131 Richard Powers, *Playground*, W. W. Norton & Company, 2025.
132 Reto Vogt, "Frendbestimmt," at *DNIP*, 2025: dnip.ch/2025/12/12/vogt-am-freitag-fremdbestimmt/
133 Danny Goodwin, "Google AI overviews drive 61% drop in organic CTR, 68% in paid," at *Search Engine Land,* 2025: searchengineland.com/google-ai-overviews-drive-drop-organic-paid-ctr-464212
Michael Savage, "AI summaries cause 'devastating' drop in audiences, online news media told," in The Guardian, 2025: theguardian.com/technology/2025/jul/24/ai-summaries-causing-devastating-drop-in-online-news-audiences-study-finds
134 In the Privacy and Permissions section of Microsoft's OneDrive, November 2025.
135 *TED en Français* podcast, 2025: open.spotify.com/episode/2RJRHLH9KudSBGT5jb5cbG
136 Owen Barcala on Bluesky, 2025: bsky.app/profile/obarcala.bsky.social/post/3lp7oevjrp22t
137 "Sam Altman on God, Elon Musk and the mysterious death of his former employee," on *The Tucker Carlson Show*, 2025: youtu.be/5KmpT-BoVf4; extract from interview adapted and condensed for space and clarity.
138 Gary Marcus, "All your data belong to us," in *MarcusOnAI*, 2025: garymarcus.substack.com/p/all-your-data-belong-to-us
139 Carissa Véliz, "How privacy can save your life," at TEDxPorto, 2025: youtube.com/watch?v=xSPRouBvgFE
140 Shannon Vallor, *The AI Mirror: How to Reclaim our Humanity in the Age Of Machine Thinking*, Oxford University Press, 2024.
141 Ethics of Example (eofe.ai).
142 Pope Leo XIV, *Message of the Holy Father to the Participants in the Builders AI Forum*, 2025: vatican.va/content/leo-xiv/it/messages/pont-messages/2025/documents/20251103-messaggio-builders-aiforum.html
143 *Social Media "Ban" or Delay FAQs*, eSafety Commissioner of the Australian Government: esafety.gov.au/about-us/industry-regulation/social-media-age-restrictions/faqs
144 Hanna Rosin, "Is this the end of kids on social media?," in *The Atlantic*, 2025: theatlantic.com/podcasts/2025/12/the-end-of-kids-on-social-media/685127/
145 *Social Media Adolescent Addiction/Personal Injury Products Liability Litigation*, US District Court for the Northern District of California, 2026: www.lieffcabraser.com/pdf/2025-11-21-Brief-dckt-2480_0.pdf
146 Brandon T. McDaniel and Jenny S. Radesky, "Technoference: Parent distraction with technology and associations with child behaviour problems," in *Child Development*, 2018: pubmed.ncbi.nlm.nih.gov/28493400/
147 Deftech (deftech.ch).
148 Atelier des Futurs (atelierdesfuturs.org).
149 *The Cognitive Threat*, Deftech Podcast, six episodes (plus a fictional instalment) available in Italian, French, and German: atelierdesfuturs.org/la-menace-cognitive (also on Spotify, Apple Podcast, and other platforms).